S. SEKOU ABC

THE secret
BEHIND THE SECRET
TONGUES SIMPLIFIED

SEKOU
PUBLISHING

The Secret behind the secret
"Tongues Simplified"

Sekou Publishing
9 Saffron Close. Maidstone. Kent. ME16 0US
publishing@sekou.me

Copyright © 2014 by Sekou Abodunrin
ISBN: 978-0-9575677-2-6
Published by Sekou Publishing. All rights reserved.

Page setting and cover design: Kenteba Kreations
contact.kenteba@gmail.com

Unless otherwise indicated, all Scripture quotations are taken from the King James Version of the Bible.

Some Scripture quotations marked (PHILLIPS) are from The New Testament in Modern English, Copyright © 1958, 1959, 1960 J.B. Phillips and 1947, 1952, 1955, 1957 The Macmillian Company, New York. Used by permission.
All rights reserved.

Some Scripture quotations marked (WEYMOUTH) are taken from Weymouth's New Testament in Modern Speech by Richard Francis Weymouth. Copyright © 1978 by Kregel Publications a division of Kregel Inc. Harper & Row Publishers, Inc., New York, New York.

Some Scripture quotations marked (TCNT) are taken from The Twentieth Century New Testament, Chicago Moody Bible Institute, 1967. Used by Permission

This book contains top secret stuff and code-breaking information that NASA does not want you to know about, so if you are reading this in a taxi cab don't read past page 6 and if you do, make sure the cabbie joins you in reading it. And yeah, ask the driver if you can take over the taxicab so you can concentrate on reading. in case there's disagreement, just pretend to be enjoying the high quality stuff on the front cover of this book after all just like everyone at NASA you are condemned to be you for the rest of your life.

DEDICATION

To the precious people of GracePlace and all those who do not want to bottle up God, we are brothers from the womb of the Word, let's keep rolling together.

To Olatee, Emiola and Alfreda - your laughter still rocks my world!

INTRODUCTION

Almost two thousand years ago, the Lord Jesus inspired the Apostle Paul to say to the Corinthians, "Now concerning spiritual gifts I will not have you ignorant". There was an undeniable flow of the supernatural in their midst but their ignorance concerning the things of the Spirit caused them to get puffed up. They did not understand the reason for those supernatural manifestations, nor did they understand how to subordinate those beautiful things of the Spirit to the law of love. Scriptural experiences are good but experiences on their own do not confer understanding otherwise Paul would not have implied that the Corinthians even with all the spiritual operations in their midst were ignorant. Only the word of God believed and acted upon destroys ignorance and delivers us from excess, pessimism and fear of the things of the Spirit. He implied that spiritual things neither need be mysterious nor confusing. We can know the ways of the Spirit.

The teaching contained within this book is intended as an introduction for someone that desires to speak in other tongues for the first time. Those that already speak in other tongues may find it equally as helpful. Understanding what speaking in other tongues involves is vital because knowledge minimizes the fear of the unknown. Wherever we substitute zeal for clarity of instruction and understanding, our practice soon starts opposing the truth and we are led down dark alleys, which result in confusion, uncertainty and excess.

In the early days, I used to rush into getting people filled with the Spirit without appreciating the simple fact that many of these people did not have a clue about what was really expected of them. People tend to fare better and can be greatly helped along when they know exactly what speaking in other tongues is and is not, how it happens and what will happen when they speak in tongues. Otherwise, I found that praying for them on a whim is usually fraught with much heat but little light and a bucket full of frustration. We often get rough with people, accusing them of unbelief when they simply have doubts that can be dispelled with clear actionable instructions.

There are far too many people that are tense when they hope to receive. There are even more tongue-talking people who retain that tension throughout most of their spiritual life. This is because they don't enter through the spiritual door of knowledge. This book is written with the aim of removing the stress from speaking in other tongues.

If, as you read through this book, you come across something that you do not completely agree with (and you might), concentrate on those things that the Spirit makes jump out to you and just press on, learn and apply what you can. We do not have to agree 100% on everything in order for us to get along. It is OK by me that you continue reading. This is written to help you, bless you but not to make a clone of anyone – follow the word, as you best know how.

It is neither your praying, shouting, screaming nor speaking in tongues that triggers change; it is what you believe about the finished works of Christ that is the key. Let your scream, shout and speaking in tongues be a release of what you know God to be.

TABLE OF CONTENTS

1

The feast is fulfilled

There are several portions of the epistles of Paul that continue to be a source of confusion amongst believers. A number of these troubling verses are in the fourteenth chapter of 1 Corinthians. It is a beneficial operating principle in the solution of many problems to assume first of all, that the root of the problem itself is often found in what everyone agrees upon. When we do agree, we often don't end up agreeing on the correct thing. This tends to be the case, that we know too much traditional wisdom, such that it reduces our ability to learn any further. It does not enable progress hence there is much unlearning to do. We must not be afraid to examine these verses. It has been said that the key to our transformation is in those verses that we all try to avoid. We aim to examine some of these scriptures in the light of the Word. We will be exploring those aspects that address the practice of speaking with other tongues. When Paul dedicated a whole chapter in his letter to the Corinthians to discussing the subject of tongues, he implied that it is not trivial.

Lets start from the beginning.

> *To whom also he shewed himself alive after his passion by many*
> *infallible proofs, being seen of them forty days, and speaking of the*
> *things pertaining to the kingdom of God: And, being assembled*
> *together with them, commanded them that they should not depart from*
> *Jerusalem, but wait for the promise of the Father, which, saith he, ye*
> *have heard of me.*
>
> [ACTS 1:3-4]

Today, the Lord Jesus is seated at the Father's right hand because He had put sin away (Heb. 1:3). However before He sat down, He spent these forty days on earth showing Himself alive to His disciples. Whatever the nature of the proof that He showed his disciples, it is obvious that Jesus did not walk around Jerusalem ministering to the sick like He used to. He could walk through walls after eating fish, disappear right out of sight but we don't see him laying hands on anyone for healing. The reason is that He no longer had a body from this earth. Therefore He had lost the authority that you could only get by having an earthly body. He is still reaching out to the sick today through you as His body on the earth. Your earthly body is invaluable to the Lord; treat it right for it is vital to your having the right to continue to exercise authority on the earth.

After Jesus' resurrection, He returned to live on the earth for forty days during which He gave the command to the disciples to wait in Jerusalem and then He sat on the Father's right hand. About six days after his seating at God's right hand, we have the events of the day of Pentecost. Thus the Lord Jesus did not immediately ascend to sit at the right hand of the Father after his resurrection; until he had first given his disciples a glimpse of what the new creation man looked and functioned like for forty days in a glorified spiritual body! He was living proof of two aspects of our redemption – a glorified body that had changed from natural to spiritual as well as evidence of the inevitability of a bodily resurrection.

Resurrection body in a fallen world

The Lord Jesus will transform our earthly bodies to resemble his own glorified body (Phil. 3:21). His is the standard of what our bodies shall be (1 Cor. 15:49). All saints shall experience a change in their bodies unto a glorious state (1 Cor. 15:51). Since He spent some time on earth in a glorified body before ascending to heaven, this makes me ask the question, "Will believers in their glorified bodies immediately leave the earth or will we spend some days on this earth in a glorified body while the earth remains in its fallen state"?

> *Jesus, when he had cried again with a loud voice, yielded up the ghost. And, behold, the veil of the temple was rent in twain from the top to the bottom; and the earth did quake, and the rocks rent; And the graves were opened; and many bodies of the saints which slept arose, And came out of the graves after his resurrection, and went into the holy city, and appeared unto many.*
>
> ### [MATTHEW 27:50-53]

This passage in Matthew is a scriptural tease but there is no doubt that Matthew wants us to take these events as historically true. He presents the resurrection of these Old Testament saints in the same context as the death and resurrection of Jesus and requires us to accept that the resurrection of these saints is as true as the resurrection of Jesus. The major difference is that Jesus is the firstborn from the dead (Col. 3:18). The implication of this is that Jesus entered into the house of death and freed those saints who were once held captive by death's power. He gives us a sense of the sequence involved when He said these events happened "after His resurrection". Since the resurrection is fact, this appearance of saints who were once dead is also fact. Just as with the case of the Lord Jesus, the bodily resurrection of the saints was characterised by revitalisation of their dead bodies, appearance to many people as well as their empty tombs. The Old Testament saints, who had died before Jesus were included in Jesus' bodily resurrection.

Who did these saints appear to? What was the criterion? Did they appear to their own families? The bible does not tell us explicitly. We know that so much resurrection power accompanied the resurrection of the Lord Jesus that it caused all the saints who died from Adam till Christ to rise out of the grave after his resurrection.

The First Resurrection

The resurrection of Jesus was the initial stage of the first resurrection and all the saints who had died up until the resurrection of Jesus were part of that phase of the first resurrection. Whatever body those saints died with would have decayed and their bones partially dissolved over time. Therefore when those saints came back to life as a result of Jesus' resurrection, it made sense that they received new bodies. Would saints who had not died in Jerusalem appear to those in Jerusalem? Again the bible does not say. I believe that it is those saints who obtained a glorified body at Jerusalem that appeared unto many in the city of Jerusalem. They did not appear as ghosts, but with real bodies. Like Jesus they would have said, "Handle me and see, for a spirit does not have flesh and bones as you see I have" (Lk. 24:39). The nail imprint on Jesus' hands and feet imply there is some continuity between His body before resurrection and afterwards. Anyway, in order for Jesus to return as the bona fide Messiah, His genetics would have to match that of Adam, Abraham and David's. How would the people at Jerusalem have validated that these resurrected saints were who they said that they were? There must have been a visible way of identifying them as Old Testament saints and whatever it was, it convinced those dwelling in Jerusalem that they had seen the saints of old. All of this happened during the Jewish Passover feast. This is one of three feasts that the Law demanded that all Jewish men come to Jerusalem for. Therefore there would have been as many Jewish men as could possibly be in Jerusalem during this period. The same crowd that demanded the death of Jesus now had ample proof of the power of His resurrection. This was not just a show of power from God but also a demonstration of His love. The things they heard from these old saints must have shaken them to the core of their being.

Did they go back to the grave?

I don't know about you but it would not make sense that after these resurrected Old Testament saints had received new bodies, that they then returned to the grave to die again in which case death would have had the last say! Those new bodies cannot die. If they did not return to the grave, where are they now? I believe that Jesus already took them up to heaven with new bodies and presented them to the Father as a first fruit offering when He ascended to heaven. They are now part of the great cloud of witnesses. They would likely have stayed around for the length of time that Jesus stayed on earth before ascending to heaven in a glorified body. I would expect that the tombs of all the Old Testament saints are empty now and that someday we will be able to verify this.

The experiences of the Lord Jesus and these saints of Old contain hints that before ascending up to meet the Lord in the air, we will receive a glorified body in the "twinkling of an eye" (1 Cor. 15:52, 1 Thess. 4:16-17). That expression "twinkling of an eye" means an atomic second. The change that transforms our bodies to a new one will happen in the twinkling of an eye. Since Jesus stayed back on earth in a new body before ascending to heaven and the Old saints also stayed behind after receiving a new body, it is my opinion that we will not immediately rush off the earth once we receive a new body. Immortality will be demonstrated in full view of those who are alive on earth at the time of our glorious change. This merciful provision could be a catalyst for the outbreak of an unprecedented revival to rake in a mighty harvest just as the Church leaves the earth. These are glimpses from the fact that the Lord stayed back 40 days after his resurrection and up till just a few days before Pentecost.

Stay in Jerusalem

These disciples had been anointed to proclaim the word to Israel during Jesus' earth walk, so they had ministered in a degree of power. The Lord Jesus Christ then told these disciples not to leave Jerusalem but to wait for the promise of the Father, which He had spoken to them about earlier. What God wanted these men to walk in and proclaim could only come about through divine vitalization by the Spirit of God. Clearly this promise that they were to wait for was nothing other than what transpired on the day of Pentecost.

The disciples could not just be anywhere of their choosing, they were commanded to be in Jerusalem. They would have been a disobedient bunch if they had left Jerusalem. This instruction was the last that the Lord gave them before His ascension to sit at the right hand of God. The simple truth is that they were not able to act on any other instruction that the Lord Jesus had given until they had first acted on this particular one. This is the only commission that they functioned under until the day of Pentecost.

As you read through the book of Acts, you discover that no Apostle or disciple communicated this instruction about waiting in Jerusalem to any other group in the bible. The instruction to wait in Jerusalem was not given to the universal church but specifically to that original company. You and I who are alive today don't have such an instruction. It was a specific instruction to a specific bunch of people.

And when the day of Pentecost was fully come, they were all with one accord in one place.

[ACTS 2:1]

Pentecost was the reason why Jesus told the disciples to wait in Jerusalem. The day of Pentecost had to be fulfilled at Jerusalem just like the Passover had been fulfilled starting with the crucifixion of Jesus outside Jerusalem (John 19:20). Everything that happened from Calvary leads right up to the events of Pentecost.

The disciples were in one place. Well, where was this place? The seemingly obvious answer to that question is that Pentecost happened in the upper room. Well, let's find out if this is so.

And when they were come in, they went up into an upper room, where abode both Peter, and James, and John, and Andrew, Philip, and Thomas, Bartholomew, and Matthew, James the son of Alphaeus, and Simon Zelotes, and Judas the brother of James. These all continued with one accord in prayer and supplication, with the women, and Mary the mother of Jesus, and with his brethren.

[ACTS 1:13-14]

The disciples were present when the Lord Jesus experienced His private rapture on Mt Olivet. They then returned to Jerusalem. This verse tells us that their hotel lodging was in the upper room in preparation for the feast of Pentecost. We also know that they continued in one accord in prayer and supplication as well.

There are enough clues about the time of the day that the disciples were filled with God.

But Peter, standing up with the eleven, lifted up his voice, and said unto them, Ye men of Judaea, and all ye that dwell at Jerusalem, be this known unto you, and hearken to my words: For these are not drunken, as ye suppose, seeing it is but the third hour of the day.

[ACTS 2:14-15]

When Peter spoke about time, he was not speaking as a westerner but as a Jew speaking to Jews. In the Psalms, Moses said, "For a thousand years in thy sight are but as yesterday when it is past, and as a watch in the night" (Ps. 90:4). This fixes the meaning of "yesterday". For the Jew, the day is over when the night watch starts. Thus when the night watch starts another day has begun. This agrees with Genesis 1:5, which says, "And the evening and the morning were the first day". The Jews believe that a day starts in the evening and ends in the morning. The pattern is not morning followed by evening. They believe that the evening-followed-by-morning pattern teaches about the upheavals of life. Evening represents the rule of darkness, gloom and sorrow while morning represents the rule of light, victory and joy. It teaches that light will overwhelm darkness. In John 11:9 when Jesus asked, "Are there not twelve hours in the day?" He meant that there are twelve hours in the day and by extension another twelve hours in the evening.

When Peter spoke of the third hour of the day on the day of Pentecost, he was referring to about 9am in the morning. The disciples became full of God around 9am on the day of Pentecost.

Where were the disciples?

The third hour must be significant, otherwise it is pointless for Peter to present this as a defence. We know that many Jewish men, from every nation under heaven had gathered at Jerusalem for the feast of Pentecost. The burning question is "Where would so many devout Jewish men be at the third hour of the day on the day of the feast of Pentecost?"

In order to answer that question, let's observe some facts about the practice of the disciples after they returned from Mt Olivet.

> *And, behold, I send the promise of my Father upon you: but tarry ye in the city of Jerusalem, until ye be endued with power from on high. And he led them out as far as to Bethany, and he lifted up his hands, and blessed them. And it came to pass, while he blessed them, he was parted from them, and carried up into heaven. And they worshipped him, and returned to Jerusalem with great joy: And were continually in the temple, praising and blessing God. Amen.*

[LUKE 24.49-53]

Luke tells us that after the Lord Jesus ascended to heaven at Bethany, the disciples dutifully returned to Jerusalem with great joy. Combining this with the records in Acts 1, it seems that the disciples interpreted Jesus' command to wait in Jerusalem as continually meeting for prayer and praise in the Jerusalem temple. So, waiting in Jerusalem meant meeting in the Jerusalem temple. Therefore, when we read that the disciples were praying, we understand that the place where they praised

God and blessed Him continually was the Jerusalem temple. Their place of prayer and continual praise was in the temple, while they lodged in the Upper Room. The disciples were continually praising and blessing God at the temple at Jerusalem and not the Upper Room.

Luke wrote both the book of Acts and Luke. So, when Luke writes in Acts 1, "these all continued with one accord in prayer and supplication", He clarifies it in Luke by saying they continued this in the temple at Jerusalem. If you will receive it, Acts 1 basically tells us that the Upper Room was their hotel, while the temple was their place of prayer, supplication, praise and blessing of God. Therefore when it says that they were in one place on the day of Pentecost, they were actually at the temple. The whole house that was filled on the day of Pentecost was the temple at Jerusalem.

We can tell from Stephen's inspired preaching that the Jews referred to the Jerusalem temple as the house.

> *But Solomon built him an house. Howbeit the most High dwelleth not in temples made with hands; as saith the prophet*

> [ACTS 7:47-48]

Thus according to Stephen, a man full of the Holy Ghost and wisdom, the house that Solomon built was actually the temple that he built at Jerusalem. So we have internal evidence in the book of Acts that the Jews referred to the temple as the house. When Luke tells us that, "suddenly there came a sound from heaven as of a rushing mighty wind, and it filled all the house where they were sitting" (Acts 2:2); that house refers to the Jerusalem temple where the feast was being administered.

The third hour of the day is the time of the morning sacrifice when the devout Jews would be gathered for prayer. As the sacrifice is made a trumpet is blown. Since they were "continually in the temple, praising God" Luke 24:53, Peter and the disciples would be at the temple to celebrate Pentecost at this hour with other devout Jews. Consider also that the 3,000 that were saved by Peter's preaching suggests a much larger crowd than the 3,000 that was present to hear Peter preach. We are not told that everyone present got saved; therefore the 3,000 were a portion of a much larger crowd. A larger area than an Upper Room would have been needed to hold this assembly. The temple at Jerusalem is also one of the few places where there would have been enough water to baptise the 3,000 men that responded to Peter's Pentecostal sermon.

God grabbed the attention of every devout Jew that day and Peter's sermon did not just begin at Jerusalem; it was spoken by a living temple within the physical temple at Jerusalem and the message of Christ as Saviour moved out from there. It is an interesting play on words on God's part to choose the natural building as the location from which He continued to accelerate the building of the spiritual building called the church.

And when the day of Pentecost was fully come, they were all with one accord in one place. And suddenly there came a sound from heaven as of a rushing mighty wind, and it filled all the house where they were sitting.

[ACTS 2:1-2]

I believe that when Luke wrote of the day coming fully, he was referring to the fact that the ceremonies of the feast of Pentecost were in full flow. Such ceremonies have to take place in the temple. The devout Jews would have congregated at the Jerusalem temple. These disciples, who shared a common belief in the resurrection of Jesus, sat huddled together. It is a most beautiful way to enjoy a service seated next to those who believe in the same things you do.

Pentecost is a Greek term meaning fifty. The Jews start daily counts from the feast of Passover. They count at the end of every evening prayer. The fiftieth count is Pentecost. The Hebrew term "Shavuot" more or less means the same thing; it is the day after seven complete weeks following the First Fruits offering of Passover. It anticipates the harvest waiting on the fields. When we read that the day of Pentecost was fully come, it means the daily count at the end of every evening prayer had reached fifty. It is 50 days after the first day of Passover (Lev. 23:15). This is why there were many devout Jews in Jerusalem during this period. The majority of these Jews would have been the very ones that the saints of Old appeared to after the resurrection of Jesus.

Hebrew scholars point out that one of the customs of the feast of Pentecost was all night reading of the Word before the day "fully comes". I love that! This means that by morning the disciples would have been saturated with God's Word. The Word and the Spirit go hand in hand. They also say that there are two times of sacrifice at the temple: at the third hour (around 9am) and the ninth hour (around 3pm) and that someone would blow a trumpet at the time of sacrifice. It is said that the third hour of the day of the feast of Pentecost corresponds to the time of the reading of passages like Exodus 19 - 20 and Ezekiel 1 - 2.

And it came to pass on the third day in the morning, that there were thunders and lightnings, and a thick cloud upon the mount, and the voice of the trumpet exceeding loud; so that all the people that was in the camp trembled. And Moses brought forth the people out of the camp to meet with God; and they stood at the nether part of the mount. And mount Sinai was altogether on a smoke, because the LORD descended upon it in fire: and the smoke thereof ascended as the smoke of a furnace, and the whole mount quaked greatly. And when the voice of the trumpet sounded long, and waxed louder and louder, Moses spake, and God answered him by a voice. And the LORD came down upon mount Sinai, on the top of the mount: and the LORD called Moses up to the top of the mount; and Moses went up.

[EXODUS 19:16-20]

And I looked, and, behold, a whirlwind came out of the north, a great cloud, and a fire infolding itself, and a brightness was about it, and out of the midst thereof as the colour of amber, out of the midst of the fire.

[EZEKIEL 1:4]

These passages describe the thunder, fire, smoke and lightning that accompanied God's appearance to Israel on Mount Sinai at the giving of the Law, as well as Ezekiel's vision of God's appearance with the sound of wind and fire. It would appear that it was as the people were reading the Word that the Spirit fell on the disciples. The keen observer will notice the agreement between the passages they were reading in Exodus and Ezekiel with the events that were unfolding before them. This fits brilliantly with the cloven tongues of fire as well as the sound of rushing wind that filled the temple on the day of Pentecost. This fulfilled the type in 2 Chronicles 5:11-14 when 120 priests dedicated Solomon's temple.

The crowd that gathered to listen were the devout Jews who had come from all over the known world of that day. God effectively guided the temple service of the day of Pentecost to its conclusion.

If it was a literal physical wind that rushed through the house it should not surprise anyone that it carries its own sound; there is nothing supernatural about that. If however, there was the sound of wind without any actual wind, that is not just supernatural but spectacular! The writer of Acts actually speaks of the sound of rushing wind and not wind itself. The sound of a rushing wind that filled the entire house means that the supernatural manifestation of sound and wind filled the whole Jerusalem temple.

The other tongues that were flowing out of the mouth of the believing ones was proof that men were now the habitation of God. God no longer provided a visitation but a habitation. He inhabits these people as the true temple of God.

All these illustrate a progressive revelation of God's glory. The glory of God walked with Adam in Genesis before the fall and later this glory descended upon Sinai from heaven. This glory later moved into the tabernacle and then the most holy place when the temple was built by Solomon. Since Pentecost that glory lives within men as the habitation of God. The true temple has changed location from Jerusalem to the heart of men indwelt by God's Spirit but the disciples as well as the other Jews were largely unaware of this fact.

Just as Jesus did not die a secret death but in the full view of the Jews, the Holy Spirit was making an entrance and it was not going to be done in secret. God wanted the people to know that a change had happened! Every devout Jew who was conversant with the Word had been given a dramatization of Ezekiel and Sinai all over again. They had proof that something new was being ushered in. God had arrested their attention and they not only had hints from the earthquake, the graves that were open, the saints of Old that rose with a new body coming into Jerusalem, the sound as of a rushing mighty wind, the cloven tongues of fire but they had actually ended up hearing about the message of Christ's resurrection from Peter. They now knew that whole portions of the Psalms were not about David but the Lord Jesus in His suffering and in His glory. Their bibles would have come alive! They would each go back to their countries marked forever by what they had seen and heard on that day of Pentecost right from within their own temple at Jerusalem. Man was now the habitation of God.

2

Cell for cell like Jesus

In order to appreciate what speaking in tongues is about, you need to familiarize yourself with some basics about man's spiritual nature.

Just before the Lord Jesus ended up on the cross He said the following,

They are not of the world, even as I am not of the world.

[JOHN 17:16]

When He said this, He had not yet gone to the cross therefore He had not yet obtained redemption for man. Jesus was speaking as a Prophet. He was calling those things that are not as though they were. This prophecy is fulfilled in the New Birth. The New Birth is a rebirth

of the human spirit so that man is of "another world". It ushers man
into the realm of God. The spirit of the born again man is born of
God. Therefore as God is not of this world, the spirit of the born
again man is not of this world.

You are from the same world and are the same class of being as the
Lord Jesus himself. You are a son of God just as Jesus is a son.

You have the spirit of His Son
*And because ye are sons, God hath sent forth the Spirit of his Son into
your hearts, crying, Abba, Father. Wherefore thou art no more a servant,
but a son; and if a son, then an heir of God through Christ.*

[GALATIANS 4:6-7]

Among the Jews, a slave cannot refer to a free man as his Abba. In
order to be able to refer to a free man as Abba, the slave must become
a free man. The point made is that the Lord Jesus has freed us from
our bondage to spiritual death, which changes our status from servants
to sons who are free men. Hence as free men we can call our Father
God our Abba. We call Him Abba Father because our status is no
longer that of servants. The God of the universe is Abba Father to
the believing one.

What is meant by, "God has sent the Spirit of his Son into your
hearts"? He does not mean that there is another voice that is crying
Abba Father. He is describing the foundation that allows us to legally
call God our Abba. The "Spirit of his Son" refers to the fact that the
Lord Jesus as the first-born from the dead is the author of the born
again nature. This born again nature within the spirit of man makes
us sons. The sending forth of the Spirit of his Son into our hearts
means that the believer is to know that he has not obtained another
version of the new nature from God. The same new nature within the
Lord Jesus is the nature within the believer so that from the spiritual
standpoint, the believer is to the Father God all that the Lord Jesus
is as son.

But he that is joined unto the Lord is one spirit.
[1 CORINTHIANS 6:17]

We are joined to the Lord. This is a spiritual joining not a physical one. The Lord is the spiritual head and we are his body. We are "one spirit". That Greek word translated "one" carries far more than the idea of similarity to the Lord. It means something singular to the absolute exclusion of any other; in other words it speaks of union. The same spiritual DNA strand that was used to build the resurrected spirit of Jesus was used to build your own spirit too. You and the Lord Jesus have the same spiritual DNA. You are chromosome-for-chromosome identical to Jesus.

The spirit of life

For the law of the Spirit of life in Christ Jesus hath made me free from the law of sin and death.

[ROMANS 8:2]

There are two related concepts here. There is the spirit of life and there is a law proceeding from that spirit of life. This spirit of life was first in Christ Jesus and it is that spirit of life that erased the effects of spiritual death by lifting Jesus out of the grip of spiritual death. When we were quickened together with the Lord Jesus (Eph. 2:5), we also received the same spirit of life. There is a law that flows from my new nature as a believer just like there was a law that flowed from my sin nature when I was dead in sins. The law of this sin nature guarantees that if a man is not born again, no matter what degree of grooming, refinement and education he receives, he will serve sin. This law chains such a man to addictions, sicknesses, diseases and a confused intellect. The law of the spirit of life is the new nature. We are to understand that at the level of a nature, we are unchained from the power of sin, from poverty of the soul as well as the darkness that once veiled our spiritual comprehension.

The born again spirit which is the nature of love is the fulfilment of the Law. We don't keep the Law by sacrifices, ordinances or practice but by possessing the new nature.

Elements of the world

But now, after that ye have known God, or rather are known of God, how turn ye again to the weak and beggarly elements, whereunto ye desire again to be in bondage? Ye observe days, and months, and times, and years.

[GALATIANS 4:9-10]

The weak and beggarly element is the Law. Speaking on behalf of the Jewish believer, Paul said that the believing Jew is no longer under bondage to the weak and beggarly elements that had put the Jew in bondage. It was as a Jew that the Lord Jesus fulfilled the whole Law, in order that the Jews could be redeemed from the Law as the foundation for salvation and sanctification, so that they could then receive the adoption of sons. All were in bondage because they could only fulfil the sacrificial aspect of the Law. No one who was bound under spiritual death could fulfil it. The unbeliever is chained in slavery to the sin nature. Only the Lord Jesus as Son and the representative Jew fulfilled the whole Law and set it aside. This was why He could set the slaves free from spiritual death.

Idol worshippers are forever trying to appease an angry God in the same way that legalistic Christians are trying to appease God by their efforts. We cannot turn to the Law for spirituality. We are made spiritual by receiving the new nature of God in the New Birth. We are to understand that nature and let it govern our walk. We see glimpses of this in the Lord Jesus. He is the only credible explanation for what the new nature is like.

He that is from above

He that cometh from above is above all: he that is of the earth is earthly, and speaketh of the earth: he that cometh from heaven is above all.

[JOHN 3:31]

As a man, the human spirit of the Lord Jesus did not originate from this world. This is because He did not have an earthly father. God was the Father of His human spirit. The spirit of the believer is also from another world. We are a new race, a new species of being brought about by the resurrection of the Lord Jesus. Jesus is the author of this life and walk. Spiritually, if there were border posts and anyone stopped your spirit at passport control, the passport you present would read "From Above".

Some folks think that God directly creates the spirit of every human at birth. I can understand that line of reasoning but this cannot be true in the light of what Jesus said in that verse. If the human spirit comes from God at birth, then all men are already from above and would therefore not need the new nature. Jesus implied that He was from above while the fellows He was addressing were not. It is when we receive eternal life at the New Birth that our human spirits come from God; that is when God becomes our heavenly Father and we become members of God's household. According to J.B Phillips, "Consider the incredible love that the Father has shown us in allowing us to be called 'children of God'—and that is not just what we are called, but what we are. Our heredity on the Godward side is no mere figure of speech" (1 John 3:1). If we had the technology at our disposal to examine the spiritual DNA of every believer, we would find that all believers test positive for possessing God's spiritual DNA. The New Birth introduces us into membership in a new spiritual species.

The history of your body is totally different from the history of your spirit. If the only realities you reckon with are biological, you will not be big on what it means to be born of God. You might even think that your body is the real you therefore you live in fear that whatever defeated your uncle will also definitely defeat you. You cannot be defeated until you empower the enemy through your beliefs. Your link to your uncle is biological and not spiritual. Your body is from this earth but your spirit is from our Father God. From God's Word, we know that whatsoever is born of God overcomes the world (1 John 4:4, 1 John 5:4). You are now a master over the forces that govern this world.

Renew your mind to the fact that you exist on more than one dimension and that there is more to you than biological facts (1 Thess. 5:23). Christians who do not understand that they have God's own DNA in their spiritual nature through the New Birth are confused about their spiritual origin. This is because they prioritise their biological origin over their spiritual origin. It is true that people who come from similar gene pools tend to carry similar weaknesses. Surely this means that since you carry God's genes you carry his strength and ability. All members of God's family have the life of God. Even if a person was a relative, if they do not have God's life, then they are not spiritual relatives. Therefore your spiritual destinies and experiences are different. Your spiritual history is summed up in two words 'in Christ'. Never accept as true of you, that which is also not true of the Lord Jesus. It is because we carry God's own spiritual DNA that He is called the Father of spirits.

The Father of spirits

Furthermore we have had fathers of our flesh which corrected us, and we gave them reverence: shall we not much rather be in subjection unto the Father of spirits, and live?

[HEBREWS 12:9]

In order to appreciate what the writer of Hebrews means by God being the Father of spirits, you must remember that until you received Christ, you fully belonged to Adam's fallen race on all three dimensions of spirit, soul and body. When you received eternal life you switched spiritual fathers. Your earthly father is no longer the source of your spirit; this is because the spirit that came from Adam passed away with the New Birth. Your earthly father however is still the father of your flesh and a DNA test will confirm this to be the case. Your spirit is from God and your body is of this earth from the first Adam. Thus as a Christian, your spirit and body are not from the same dimension.

When the writer of Hebrews says that God is the Father of spirits, he means that just as with any father, God is the Father of those who are His own children. His children are those in whom God's seed remains (1 John 3:9). They have the essence and DNA of God. These spirits, that God is the Father of, are the spirit of just men made perfect through the New Birth. The unsaved man's human spirit comes from Adam's fall. He does not mean that God is the father of the spirit of the unbelieving one.

The New Birth is really a spiritual birth that ends your spiritual membership in the family of the first Adam while causing you to become a son of God. Adam gave you your biological body through your earthly father while in the New Birth God gives you a brand new spirit. A day is coming that you will also get a new body (Phil. 3:21) but for now you carry the body that is derived from the first Adam (1 Cor. 15:49). This is not the first time that we find the concept of a human being having a spirit from heaven while possessing an earthly body. At His birth, the Lord Jesus Christ had the life of God within His spirit, which was supplied by God. This was housed within an earthly body supplied by Mary.

The body that we now have is not exactly the same as Adam had originally before sin entered. There were no genetic defects in Adam before he fell but afterwards death started working in his body creating various mutations and diseases which he then passed on to his generations (Gen. 5:3). Today, we carry various degrees of weakness in our bodies. Hence, the body is currently perishable, mortal, and weak. One day soon, death will be swallowed up in victory, when the body becomes imperishable, immortal and glorious because sin will be removed from the body and the life of God will sustain it (1 Cor. 15:54).

> *For we have not an high priest which cannot be touched with the feeling of our infirmities; but was in all points tempted like as we are, yet without sin.*
>
> [HEBREWS 4:15]

Mary had a fallen body; therefore she could only birth a fallen body. All the children she gave birth to would have a fallen body since everything produces after its kind. This means that the Lord Jesus as a true son of Mary walked on earth with a fallen body. This was why He could be tempted in all points as we are. You see, the Lord Jesus was not tempted as Adam was, but as we are. Since we are tempted in a fallen body, He was tempted in a fallen body too. In His humanity, He was tempted in all points as we were but unlike the believer today, He learnt to rely on His spiritual nature by using the life of God to reign over the flesh. This is the way we are to reign over sin today also.

And the Holy Ghost descended in a bodily shape like a dove upon him, and a voice came from heaven, which said, Thou art my beloved Son; in thee I am well pleased. And Jesus himself began to be about thirty years of age, being (as was supposed) the son of Joseph, which was the son of Heli

[LUKE 3:22-23]

It was when the Holy Ghost descended upon the Lord Jesus that He became anointed with power. This did not happen until He was thirty years old. This shows that at least for the first thirty years of His life, without the anointing of the Holy Spirit, and just by relying on the presence of God's life within His human spirit, He proved the power within the nature of God's life within His own human spirit to cause Him to walk as a godlike man. He was always God but He laid that aside (Heb. 2:7). He was godlike on earth. He was not godlike because He was God but because He learnt to rely on the same spirit of life that the believer has because he is born from above. If we will depend on the spirit of life and the law of the spirit of life, we will also walk godlike in the earth — absolute masters over the flesh, the world and satan himself.

You are to believe that in your spirit you are cell for cell like Jesus. The enemy will tempt you with thoughts of doubt in your mind (2 Cor. 11:3). He wants to convince you to become a double-minded man. If you yield to that temptation, you become unstable in all your ways (Jas.

1:8). Doubting God's Word is the root of all forms of instability.

For verily I say unto you, That whosoever shall say unto this mountain,
Be thou removed, and be thou cast into the sea; and shall not doubt in
his heart, but shall believe that those things which he saith shall come to
pass; he shall have whatsoever he saith.

[MARK 11:23]

Greek scholars point out that the phrase "shall not doubt in his heart" is written in the passive voice. Thus the man who is commanding this mountain to move is receiving the doubt. This should therefore be translated as "shall not receive doubt in his heart". We must not always take it that heart and spirit are equivalent. Heart in this case, refers to the soul and not to the spirit, for the recreated spirit, being born of God, cannot doubt or promote instability (1 John 3:9).

Since this doubt is received, doubt is not native to the heart of the believer. It is a temptation to not believe. This means that though you might hear the voice of doubt within, you are to remember that it is from outside of you and you don't have to yield to the temptation to doubt. Doubt is usually received in the mind after we believe the promise of God. The intention is to cause us to withdraw from the Word. Stand fast in the Word and let the consciousness of who you are in the spirit begin to dominate your walk. Before long, your faith in God's Word will cause you to start seeing what you believe. Since the power of life and death is in your words (Prov. 18:20), use the words of your mouth to minister death to the doubts that the enemy is sending into your thoughts.

3

Spiritual Anatomy

And the LORD God formed man of the dust of the ground, and breathed into his nostrils the breath of life; and man became a living soul.

[GENESIS 2:7]

There are animals on earth. God made these animals as well as the body of Adam from the dust of the ground (Gen. 2:19). On a chemical, biological and soulish level, there is a lot that is similar between Adam's body and the animal creation.

Man though has a component that animals of the earth do not have since God breathed into man's nostrils the breath of life. God passed from himself into Adam some of God's spiritual qualities and substance. God never put his own breath into the animals. Just as there are animals on the earth plane, there are animals in heaven. For example, Elijah's transport out of this earth was in a chariot pulled by horses. Those are not biological horses (2 Kings 2:11). There are horses in heaven (Rev. 19:11) and if this is so, then there must be other animals in heaven too. The animals in heaven were not made from the dust of the ground but from heavenly substance (Gen. 2:1). This earth is a copy of heaven and there will be a new heaven as well as a new earth (Rev. 21:1). I believe that when God says from his throne, "Behold I make all things new" (Rev. 21:5), it includes animals on the new earth that will be created afresh. Animals don't pass from earth to heaven. At death, animals simply return to the earthly substances.

Speaking of this superior spiritual component in man, Peter said;

> *But let it be the hidden man of the heart, in that which is not corruptible,
> even the ornament of a meek and quiet spirit, which is in the sight of
> God of great price.*
>
> [1 PETER 3:4]

The human spirit is man's fundamental nature and it is the lamp of the Lord. The human spirit is referred to as the hidden man. It is the man within the heart. In the born again man, the spirit is to have the pre-eminence. Our recreated spirit should be the dominant aspect of our constitution. In many Christians, the spirit remains hidden therefore they doubt its power. Some even think that all that they are is biological, chemical and soulish but man's spiritual component, though mainly hidden in most people is the true definition of what man is. There is a lot about you that is not obvious to your own eye until you let God's Word show it to you. From God's perspective, the true man is the hidden man of the heart. Your spirit is superior to your soul and your body. It is with our body that we contact the material world, while at the same time the hidden man of the heart links us up with the many dimensions of the invisible spiritual realm. The human spirit is capable of infinitely more than his soul and in turn the soul has more abilities than the body.

The body and beyond

It is mind boggling the variety that we have in the biological realm alone. For example, while humans move around by sight, not all animals move around by sight. Dolphins navigate by bouncing sound waves around and with the feedback from those sound waves they map out their territory in superb detail. Scientists refer to this as echolocation. It is equivalent to "seeing" through sounds. When pregnant women visit the gynaecologist and they are given a scan of their baby within the womb, those pictures are produced by sound waves. We have come to trust these images of babies within the womb produced purely by sound when the physical eyes by itself cannot see beyond the protruding belly.

I once read of a completely blind boy in the United States who taught himself from the age of three to "see" with the sounds he heard with his ears. As he walked, he located objects by making continuous clicking sounds with his tongue. He would then use the echoes that bounced off these objects to create detailed mental images of his environment and adjust his direction as necessary. The marvel of it is that this boy was born with proper function in both eyes but lost both to cancer as a little boy. He had a phenomenal mother who repeatedly told him that he had no impossibilities, so the little boy took his mother's words to heart and from the tender age of three he taught himself to navigate around by using the clicking sounds he made with his tongue. This young boy had so developed this sense of sound that he could walk into your presence and tell whether you accepted or rejected him. He had compensated for the loss of his sense of seeing by developing his sense of hearing to such a degree that he could "see" through sounds. If in that sense we can see with our natural ears, it is marvellous the level of adaptation that the human brain is capable of by God's design. Yet with all that, the human body is no match for the human spirit.

Consider also that there are various accounts of clinically brain-dead people, who when resuscitated come back to tell what happened in their out of body experience when according to medicine they were already dead. Many recount in vivid detail, the things that were going on in the hospital room while they were brain dead as well as what the doctors were trying to do in attempting to revive them. They also share the thoughts flowing through them while they watched the panorama unfolding before their eyes in the midst of all that pandemonium in the intensive care unit. The thing is, how are these people able to recall these events when their brain cells are not functional? What senses did they use to interact with the environment and take in all that information? Those thoughts are not stored in the brain since they were brain dead. They recalled those thoughts independent of the brain. All these point to the existence of components in man that are beyond biology. The bible gives us insight into this spiritual component in man.

Spiritual senses

The Lord Jesus gives some thought provoking insight concerning some attributes of the spirit of man in his retelling of conversations beyond the grave that took place in his account of the rich man and Lazarus.

> *There was a certain rich man, which was clothed in purple and fine linen, and fared sumptuously every day: And there was a certain beggar named Lazarus, which was laid at his gate, full of sores, And desiring to be fed with the crumbs which fell from the rich man's table: moreover the dogs came and licked his sores. And it came to pass, that the beggar died, and was carried by the angels into Abraham's bosom: the rich man also died, and was buried; And in hell he lift up his eyes, being in torments, and seeth Abraham afar off, and Lazarus in his bosom. And he cried and said, Father Abraham, have mercy on me, and send Lazarus, that he may dip the tip of his finger in water, and cool my tongue; for I am tormented in this flame. But Abraham said, Son, remember that thou in thy lifetime receivedst thy good things, and likewise Lazarus evil things: but now he is comforted, and thou art tormented. And beside all this, between us and you there is a great gulf fixed: so that they which would pass from hence to you cannot; neither*

can they pass to us, that would come from thence. Then he said, I pray thee therefore, father, that thou wouldest send him to my father's house: For I have five brethren; that he may testify unto them, lest they also come into this place of torment. Abraham saith unto him, They have Moses and the prophets; let them hear them. And he said, Nay, father Abraham: but if one went unto them from the dead, they will repent. And he said unto him, If they hear not Moses and the prophets, neither will they be persuaded, though one rose from the dead.

[LUKE 16:19-31]

Death was not inevitable for Adam until he brought it upon himself through disobedience (Rom. 5:19). His death was conditional upon his sin. Subsequently, all that are born of Adam have been subject to physical death (1 Cor. 15:21). As you read about the rich man and Lazarus, remember that Abraham, Lazarus and this rich man had died and were buried on the earth.

While conversations between Abraham and the rich man are documented, we can only assume that Lazarus and Abraham must have talked, though we are not told about the manner of conversation that they had. Since Abraham is having conversations with the spirit of the rich man whose body is buried but whose soul is intact, it is not the body that gives to man the power to have conversations.

This story illustrates that beyond the grave, the spirit of the rich man was still dominated by the way he reasoned before he died on earth. He thought that he could still send Lazarus on errands but was unaware that it was impossible for Lazarus to go preach on earth; this shows his limited understanding of the spiritual world. Death does not confer on anyone higher spiritual intelligence. Abraham was more familiar with the operations of life beyond the grave than the rich man was. There are varying degrees of comprehension beyond the grave. Abraham likely had a deeper comprehension than even Lazarus. We all do not suddenly come to the same depth and level of knowledge. We will all know more, but some people will know beyond others as they develop spiritually at a different rate.

Abraham's statement, "If they hear not Moses and the prophets" shows that the rich man and his brothers lived under the Law of Moses. Since Abraham had been dead for about 250 years by the time Moses was born, the rich man lived long after Moses' death; the rich man was not in any way a contemporary of Abraham. Interestingly the rich man seemed to instantly recognize Abraham for he called him "Father Abraham". Such recognition cannot be a function of memory, but a characteristic of the human spirit. Abraham also implied that he remained aware of important spiritual events taking place on earth like the giving of the Law and the prophecies of the prophets hundreds of years after his death. Abraham would not know the colour of their Chariots for those things have no spiritual value.

Abraham said that there was a great gulf fixed between the rich man and himself and the rich man saw Abraham afar off. This shows that there was a great distance involved and yet when the rich man and Abraham conversed, both instantly understood each other. The rich man was not the only one in hell and others must have been conversing. Therefore, how did they have a conversation where both heard one another? Was every other occupant of hell silent during this discourse? If not, how could these two maintain a conversation across the great divide? It could not have been verbal. This is a conversation between spirits. Spiritual communion is on a higher level beyond the limitations of earthly language. It is almost as though they communicated beyond spoken language, in much the same way a man would look across the room at a woman he is in love with and without words he could "speak" volumes to her. It would appear that Abraham and the rich man understood each other via spiritual impressions and thoughts. Thoughts and impressions are more accurate forms of spiritual communion and they are instantly recognized and interpreted in the spirit realm.

Abraham said to the rich man, "son remember …". In calling him a son we know that Abraham knew that he was genetically related to the rich man though both ended up on different sides of the divide. You see, a man is not saved just because he is a Jew. Abraham perfectly expected the man to be able to recall events from his time on earth. The grave does not wipe our memories and since the brain was dissolved in the dust of the earth, it must mean that there is a non-biological component in man aside from the brain that stores memories which can then be remembered beyond the grave. The fact that Abraham expected the rich man to "remember" implies that thoughts existed in the unseen realm so that even when the natural storage in their brain is dead, these thoughts live on. The fact that the rich man remembered that he had five wayward brothers on earth, and that Lazarus was a man he could send on errands show that there is some continuity of memory that is carried over from the rich man's time on the earth. This is understandable since memory is a basic element of personality. This establishes that beyond the grave we are not different people, but the same people marvelously relocated and transformed. Heaven does not erase our person.

It was almost as though Abraham could tell the rich man's history by observing him. He could tell what manner of life both the rich man and Lazarus had on earth as well as the kind of desires that ruled them. This is not unique to Abraham. It is likely the rich man would have been able to tell the history of Abraham also but maybe not in as much depth as Abraham. The rich man's torments are clearly not physical since his body was buried in the grave. Those torments were non-biological in nature. The degree of torment would diminish his spiritual intelligence since he did not know for example that he could not send Lazarus on any errand.

The ability to remember shows that thoughts do not stop existing after death. Since the brain is buried in the grave, the implication is that thoughts exist outside the brain. Your thoughts will outlive your physical body. The soul of this rich man retained his memories as well as facts about the man and his family on earth. He remembered how many brothers he had on earth and he still recognized Lazarus. These are functions of his soul. Thus we can tell that the spirit retains the soul at death. The soul goes wherever the spirit goes. The soul is so tied to the spirit before and after death that only God's Word has the power to separate soul and spirit. Even when we leave our bodies in death, spirit and soul will go together.

When Abraham said to the rich man, "Lazarus is comforted", the comfort relates to how he deals with the memory of unpalatable spiritual events before the grave. You see, if there was no memory of the unpalatable things, what would be the need for, purpose of, or nature of the comfort concerning them? This means that through the impartation of comfort, Lazarus' memory was properly restored. He could recall without the pain. His comfort was not a false bliss based on ignorance of things gone before. It would appear that in Heaven, those who endured bad things on earth are comforted for them (Luke 16:25). We can look at things from a wiser perspective as we submit ourselves to God's wisdom.

The eyes that the rich man lifted up in hell are the eyes of his spirit man since his biological eyes were buried in the grave. Thus, the spirit man has eyes. Interestingly when he lifted up his spiritual eyes he saw Abraham. Thus the function of the spiritual eye at least matches those of the biological eyes. Since he saw Abraham afar off, we can tell that beyond the grave and in the spirit realm, we experience spiritual distance and perspective. This means that there is time. It does not appear that man can exist outside time, space and distance. The spirit man covers greater distances through impressions and thoughts but distance remains.

The rich man requested that Abraham send Lazarus to dip the tip of his finger in water and cool the rich man's tongue. Since Lazarus is dead and buried, he is not referring to Lazarus' biological finger that had decomposed to dust in Judea. Therefore Lazarus' spirit has fingers while the rich man's spirit has a tongue that can be cooled as well as a spiritual mind capable of remembering things. The spiritual tongue is capable of sensations. The function of the spiritual eyes, fingers and tongue are similar to that of the biological eye, fingers and tongue. The anatomy of the human spirit is surely not a set of eyes, fingers and a tongue dangling out of nothingness. These parts must be connected in a way that's similar to the arrangement of our biological anatomy. The physical world is a mirror of the spiritual world.

The spirit man has a real anatomy that would not only have fingers, a tongue and eyes but also a mind, ears and legs. This implies that there are other inner senses and that there is a spirit characteristic corresponding to each biological sense in our physical body. You could say that my spiritual neck fills up my physical neck, just like my spiritual tongue and eyes fill up my physical tongue and eyes respectively. My spiritual brain also fills up my natural brain and it is within this spiritual brain that you have the soul.

The story shows that the inner senses are more enduring and will outlast the outer senses. The inner senses are not visible to the outer eye but are in fact eternal. Our outer senses were built as copies of the senses of the spirit man. The spirit man has senses like the human body has senses and the spiritual senses are for contacting the spiritual realm.

We do not acquire spiritual senses at death. It's just that during the normal course of the day, the level of distraction in our natural minds usually blocks our consciousness of the spiritual senses. When we dream, these inner senses are more dominant than our outer senses because our conscious minds are not in the way (Job 33:14 - 16). As we allow God's peace rule our hearts, we also become aware of our spiritual senses. The majority of us go through our conscious moments totally oblivious of the sensations that our inner senses are broadcasting. There are certain activities like speaking in tongues and meditating God's word that cause our consciousness of our spiritual senses to be more dominant than the senses in our outer man.

It is our born again spirit man that speaks in tongues (1 Cor. 14:14) as the indwelling Holy Spirit generates the language by giving the utterance (Acts 2:4), which we then speak. Those who have God's

DNA in the new creation are given a new language for their spirit man. This is what Paul referred to as the tongues of Angels (1 Cor. 13:1).

Only the born again spirit can speak in tongues. The spirit of the one who is not born again communicates but it cannot be tongues. Abraham could not have been speaking in tongues because he had righteousness on credit; he was not born again. Jesus had not yet died for sins, therefore the born again experience was not available for any man at the time of Abraham's conversation with the rich man. Another reason Abraham could not have been speaking in tongues to the rich man is that when we speak in tongues, the direction of communication is either from man to God or when combined with interpretation of tongues the direction is from God back to man. It is not designed as a means of one man speaking to another.

Speaking in tongues is yielding your physical tongue to your spiritual tongue so you can speak spiritual utterances generated within your spirit by the Holy Ghost. The Holy Ghost generates this utterance within your spiritual mind, which resides within your natural mind. The utterances that become tongues are not accessible through the biological ear but through the spiritual ear. You can hear other people speak in tongues through your biological ear but you don't hear the Holy Spirit supplying the utterance to you in your biological ear. As you exercise these faculties of your spirit man, you'll come to pick up the sounds, images and impressions that will become tongues with your spiritual senses. Some people even see the words with their spiritual eye in an inner vision.

Spiritual sense of hearing

So then faith cometh by hearing, and hearing by the word of God.

[ROMANS 10:17]

The most basic sense of the human spirit is the sense of hearing. This is the case as it is through the hearing of faith that we received eternal life. Hearing and speaking out our faith develops this spiritual sense of hearing. In Genesis, the Holy Ghost knew God's thoughts but there was no creative act until God spoke words (Gen. 1:2). The Holy Spirit does not act on our thoughts; He is commissioned to bring our words to pass. The words that we speak out of our mouths release our dominion and activate the Holy Ghost to manifest our words. It is in order to develop this spiritual sense of sound that God's Word places tremendous emphasis on what we hear. As you continue to hear the Word, you are tuning your inner sense of hearing so that you can hear more accurately into the realm of God. It is because we understand the primal nature of this sense of hearing that we can control what we say.

> *Speaking to yourselves in psalms and hymns and spiritual songs, singing and making melody in your heart to the Lord;*
> ### [EPHESIANS 5:19]

There is a collective melody that is carried within every language on earth. It is as though the language of any society carries its triumphs, joys and pains. Our new society in God also has sounds and melodies; which is why God encourages us to speak to ourselves until we make melody in our hearts. Thus sounds whether spoken, chanted, sang or mumbled all carry a signature melody. Speaking in tongues for example is a language and it is a melody that we speak or sing. When we speak in tongues, we are tapping into and releasing the rich vein of inner music placed there by God. God Himself is musical (Zeph. 3:17) and wants us to tap into His musical nature, which He deposited in us at the New Birth. It is part of our spiritual development to learn to project that music out; this way we remain in sync with God.

Spiritual communication

> *But as it is written, Eye hath not seen, nor ear heard, neither have entered into the heart of man, the things which God hath prepared for them that love him. But God hath revealed them unto us by his Spirit:*

for the Spirit searcheth all things, yea, the deep things of God.

[1 CORINTHIANS 2:9-10]

God does not communicate through our biological senses but through our spiritual senses. He does this via revelation. Divine revelation is hearing and seeing through the inward senses of the human spirit. It is the spiritual equivalent of hearing and seeing biologically. Divine revelation is from God's Spirit to our spirit primarily through thoughts and impressions. Revelation imparts insight but it is not directly through the knowledge of any human language itself; rather the meaning and thoughts of God are communicated directly and instantaneously. God does not speak in human language even though we seem to hear God in the language that we are conversant with in our natural mind.

When you appear to hear God speak in a human language, it is because your spirit first understands it in a manner beyond language and then conveys it to your soul in a language that your mind understands. When you hear God speak to you in your vernacular, it is not that He actually verbalised your vernacular. He communicates (spiritually) to your spirit man at a depth too high for the human language to transmit. Your human spirit then steps this down for the benefit of your intellect in your everyday vernacular. Therefore at the point it registers on your soul, you are convinced that God spoke your vernacular.

Divine revelation is an impartation of experience and knowledge. It is like data exchange between two mobile phones, except that while this mobile illustration explains the idea of the flow of facts, it does not show the transfer of the full experience and sensations involved with divine revelation.

It appears that if there was a way to examine our thoughts, we would find that our thoughts store and transfer our spiritual history the same way blood carries the biological history of a man's body.

Not all the thoughts in our heart are from God. Thoughts are not our battle but every time we experience resistance or assistance from the spirit realm thoughts show up. There are various sources for the thoughts that float through you and many of these thoughts attempt to interfere with the thoughts of God that are already in you. The love of the Father in you causes you to know who God is and who you are in the spirit. When you know who you are and you persist in speaking God's Word, you start taking God's love thoughts, which filter out those interferences out of your heart. It will cause you to hit the exact frequency of God's thoughts.

4

The Joint

Animals have a body and a capacity to express emotions therefore they have a soul as well. The souls of animals are tied to their bodies. In man, the soul is additionally linked to his spirit. It is because our souls are tied to our spirits that the soul has eternal qualities. The soul of man is not like the soul of animals. In animals, there is no spirit therefore the soul is the highest component. Man is a spirit being, who has a soul.

For the word of God is quick, and powerful, and sharper than any twoedged sword, piercing even to the dividing asunder of soul and spirit, and of the joints and marrow, and is a discerner of the thoughts and intents of the heart.

[HEBREWS 4:12]

The soul of man is so joined to the human spirit that God's Word is the only substance in existence that can separate soul from spirit.

If you are not scripturally taught, you will attribute to the spirit those things that the bible says belong to the soul.

The soul of man is compared to joints. Joints join two parts together. In this case, the soul of man is the joint between the human spirit and the body. The reason why some Christians are "spiritual" and others are "carnal" has to do with the nature of the joint delivered through the soul. All Christians start out as new-born spiritual babies (1 Pet. 2:2) who are self-conscious and depend upon others for everything but they support no one. New-born babies then develop into spiritual or carnal but whether spiritual or carnal all have the same righteousness, holiness and sonship (1 Cor. 1:30). A spiritual Christian grew from being self-conscious to becoming a Christ-conscious one whose soul agrees with his reborn spirit because it prioritises the Word above all else. A carnal Christian is a spiritual baby whose soul does not prioritise the Word instead it teams up with the body and is ruled by selfishness. Churches have issues to deal with because the carnal Christians think they are spiritual hence they make carnality look normal. There is no selfish person who is spiritually mature. Our wills are like a hinge that swings our soul into self-consciousness or Christ-consciousness. Our will acts as joints to support our spirit or our body.

Try to visualise this: There are spiritual deposits that want to flow from your spirit through the mind of Christ to your body but your soul mounts a resistance before it can get from your spirit to your body. The will is like the soldier guarding that gate. The gate is the intellect. Your will swings the gate open for the life within your spirit to pour forth into your body or otherwise for the death of the world to pour into your body.

We have shown that the human spirit has its own senses. For example, the spirit has a spiritual mouth just like the body has a biological mouth. When your spirit wants to speak, it does not just grab your biological mouth and force it to move. Your biological mouth is under the control of your body for it is a part of your body. There is a need for a joining of your spirit and your body in order for your spirit to "move" your mouth. Since praying in tongues involves your spirit (1 Cor. 14:14) and your biological tongue, this joint is needed – this is why you have to will to do so. This is what Paul means when he says, "I will pray with the spirit and I will pray with the understanding" (1 Cor. 14:15). Thus speaking in tongues prove that the anatomy of man spans three dimensions. The human spirit is speaking and the will, which is a function of the soul, is using the mouth to voice the spirit.

If as a result of the teaching I have been exposed to, I am prejudiced against speaking in tongues, the prejudice is in my soul. In that prejudiced state, my will swings the hinges such that my mouth will not be available to speak out any words in tongues, no matter the degree of utterance that the Holy Spirit provides. In this case, the problem is never about the availability of the Spirit but how yielded the human will is.

Love removes the noise

There is no fear in love; but perfect love casteth out fear: because fear hath torment. He that feareth is not made perfect in love.

[1 JOHN 4:18]

Fear has torment. Love and fear are opposites. Hell is simply the perfection of fear. It is the fear in our soul that attracts the wrong type of spirits who inject the wrong thoughts and desires into our thought stream. Dwelling on these wrong thoughts empower them to become strong desires (Jas. 1:14). The evil spirits feed off the strength of these desires to inspire us to act wrong. These spirits derive their energy from our fear. It is as we yield to the power of God's love in us that we become less penetrable by these thoughts, which try to distort God's original thought flowing through our inner life. The love of God casts out fear and whatever casts out our fear purifies our thoughts to perceive God's thoughts that are broadcasted to us.

Those whose hearts are kept pure by the power of God's love shall see God, hear God and sense God's impressions. God is always able and willing to help us whether we prioritise his love or not. We will find though that when we don't prioritise His love we hinder ourselves from seeing, sensing or receiving His help.

The love of God is effective for cancelling out the various sources of noise in our lives until the thoughts of God become the most dominant thoughts within. One of the hallmarks of real spiritual growth is developing your ability to decipher which of the thoughts in you at present originated from God. A will that is set against the spirit hinders us from becoming experts at locating and isolating these limiting thoughts, which generate a lot of noise in the believer.

The power of the love of God that is shed abroad in your heart is the filter that cancels out all the noise that is trying to distort God's communion with you. God pours that love into your spirit and your will permits that love to overflow from the spirit into the rest of your constitution. As you stay love-of-God-conscious you purify your heart and set your will to align with your spirit. Too many Christians want to hate like the devil and yet remain calm like God. They are so highly developed in opposing the love of God that they have robbed themselves of divine boldness and the clarity that belongs to them as believers.

The grace of our Lord Jesus Christ be with your spirit. Amen.
[PHILEMON 1:25]

The grace of the Lord Jesus is with our spirits. That grace is needed in the soul and in the body. It is through a will that swings in favour of the spirit that the grace within our spirits overflows into our everyday lives in the natural world. When the mind is not renewed, there is a great gulf between the soul and the spirit. This leads to civil war within the believer (Gal. 5:17).

We can keep asking God to pour more grace into our lives but His grace is supplied to our spirit and is multiplied in our lives as we gain knowledge of His Word (2 Pet. 1:2). The knowledge of God's Word renews our minds and also corrects our decision-making! Much more than the knowledge gained, our decision to go with the Word causes the resistance in our wills to become less and less until over time any barrier between our spirit and soul evaporates because the will is more trusting of the spirit man.

Pulling down the walls between soul and spirit

In majority of Christians, the will is like a thick wall preventing the spirit from overflowing into the mind, emotions and the body. This thick wall was built over a lifetime of mistrusting the spirit when it was dead in sins. A dead spirit promotes death. We therefore needed a thick wall between our spirits and our souls when we were not born again. You don't want the soul and spirit of an unbeliever in agreement. People whose wills readily cooperate with their spiritually dead spirits see nothing wrong with killing millions of people. We know them as the despots of history. They serve as clear examples of why the soul of man must be unhinged from the spirit of man outside Christ.

Civilised societies are those who enforce this "unhinging" through grooming in etiquette. Our educational systems are largely the tools we use to unhinge the soul from the spirit and train ourselves to mistrust the human spirit. Spiritually dead men who understand the privileges that come with disregarding the spirit largely designed our education system. They were shunning the spiritually dead human spirit and rightly so. Thus the education we receive in our institutions as well as the grooming of society largely trains us to ignore that dead spirit by enthroning the soul. It systematically trains us to erect thick walls between our soul and our spirit. It unhooks the soul from the spirit of man who is dead in sins. The more educated we are, the thicker the wall imposed by the will. It hooks the soul of man into the system of the world. The man demonstrates the illusion of progress but his spirit is still as deadly. The whole man is spirit, soul and body but functionally the spirit is dethroned and ignored. The natural man functions like a soul and body. Man is living by his soul and not by his spirit (Eph. 4:17). Every unbeliever needs to have a thick wall protecting their soul from their spirit. Shielding their soul from their spirit is the right thing otherwise the earth will be like hell.

Interestingly, when man gets born again, it's his spirit that becomes completely new. The grace of the Lord Jesus is made available to that recreated spirit but his will still keeps erecting the thick wall! That wall is the reason for carnal Christians and selfishness. The spirit does not need to be born again and again. Once born again, it is the wall erected by the will to protect the soul from the spirit that must come down through the renewing of the mind to God's Word.

Christians who have thick walls protecting their soul from their spirit are shielding themselves from the answer! Even as they ignore their spirits, they hear the truth of God's Word with their mind but their will remains hardened like concrete against the spirit. They are not yielded to the spirit man. Therefore, they are not able to fully enter into spiritual things nor are they able to receive the overflow of life and power flowing out of the spirit.

The rest of our spiritual walk is mostly renewing our minds and more importantly learning to deliberately and on purpose yield our will to the recreated spirit and the Holy Spirit. As we practice this deliberate choosing of the Word, the thick wall imposed by the will begins to thin. We must learn to live by the recreated spirit.

5

The Reborn Spirit Knows

The candle is lit

And these are they which are sown on good ground; such as hear the word, and receive it, and bring forth fruit, some thirtyfold, some sixty, and some an hundred. And he said unto them, Is a candle brought to be put under a bushel, or under a bed? and not to be set on a candlestick?

[MARK 4:20 - 21]

J esus said that if we understand this parable, we have the keys for grasping the operation of the kingdom of God (Mk. 4:13). The Lord Jesus uses this teaching to illustrate the effect of the implanted Word in the heart of man. In the natural, the farmer starts the cycle of harvest by planting seeds in the ground. There is a parallel between the farmer and the believer. According to this parable, the

Word of God is the seed. We plant the seed of God's Word into our heart by hearing the spoken Word.

We understand that cucumbers will produce more cucumbers after its specific kind (Gen. 1:11). Cucumbers cannot produce chili pepper.

We also know that God's Word is the original from which all the created things derive their existence (John 1:1 - 4).

Therefore the Word of God is a unique seed, for it is the universal seed for everything.

God's Word has the unique characteristic of being the only seed that can become anything in both the spiritual and natural realms of life. Give God's Word the first place in your life because God's Word is to you, what the seed is to the Farmer.

We are to know the mysteries of the kingdom of God. These mysteries are meant to become knowledge for those that believe. You see, God can be known with precision. The spiritual baby relates to everything as mysterious, while those who are maturing in God harvest more and more of those mysteries as knowledge. God does not give out presents celebrating how many things remain as mysteries to us.

Spiritual death dulls the spiritual mind and limits its comprehension quite drastically. Ordinarily, these disciples would not have understood anything that Jesus was saying because they had the nature of spiritual death within their spirits. Thankfully, He gives us keys for unlocking the parable.

Then quite unexpectedly, right in the middle of His sermon on the seed and its sower He asked, "Is a candle brought to be put under a bushel, or under a bed? and not to be set on a candlestick?"

He brings up the idea of a candle right in the middle of His teaching about the seed! He is illustrating that we should display our candles so that we can benefit from the light that it projects in the midst of darkness. He expects us to understand the relationship between the farmer planting seeds for harvest and a candle that is set on the candlestick.

Since Jesus spoke this right in the middle of a parable, we know that He was still continuing to use the teaching aid of a parable. He was not telling us to go looking for literal candles. Thankfully, God gave Solomon some revelation about the allegorical meaning of a candle.

> *The spirit of man is the candle of the LORD, searching all the inward parts of the belly.*
>
> [PROVERBS 20:27]

We know from Solomon's insight that the human spirit is the candle of the Lord. The human spirit is God's light bulb that He uses to give you light. So, when the Lord Jesus refers to the candle, He is referring to the human spirit. The Lord Jesus is the light that lights the candle of the world (John 8:12). He is the light of salvation (John 1:9). The Lord lights our candle by giving the life of Jesus as light to our spirit man. Therefore, when the Psalmist said, "For thou wilt light my candle: the LORD my God will enlighten my darkness" (Psalm 18:28), he meant that God would provide salvation to the spirit of man and this would cause man's spirit to have light.

The candle under the bushel describes the condition of the human spirit hidden in spiritual death and veiled in darkness without light. The candle set on a candlestick describes the human spirit elevated by God's divine life out of that place of darkness into the primal place of pre-eminence in human affairs. The translation out of darkness is so that the spirit of man is given the first place.

The human spirit needs to first receive light, before it can then give light. That light is the light of life (John 1:4) which is the new nature proceeding from the born again spirit. The candle set upon a candlestick describes God lighting our candle, so that we know things supernaturally. Don't ignore the light in your candle.

The parable teaches that those who are translated out of darkness by receiving the new birth are to use the seed of God's Word, planted in the soul, as the weaponry for harvest of illumination, direction and clarity for "the entrance of thy word giveth light" (Ps. 119:130). This harvest of light comes thirty, sixty and hundred fold because of the varying ability of the soul to cooperate with the implanted Word. The soul receives the vitalization of God through the implanted Word. As you feed the soul on the Word, it becomes a better companion of the recreated spirit. It is because we have a soul that we get better at receiving the leadership of God through the recreated human spirit.

In other words, the parable teaches that we, whose spirits have been recreated and whose candles have received the light of life, should take the Word of God as subject matter for our education in God. Then, as we exercise our spirit and give the recreated spirit the primal place in our life, the light within that candle swings open the door of revelation. That light projected out of our spirits becomes the illumination that leads our soul out of that experience of "not knowing" into the fullness of clarity concerning God's will. The recreated spirit, as the candle upon the candlestick, is the primary weapon God uses to get you to progress from mysteries into concise knowledge in every sphere of your life. The reborn spirit is a weapon of mass revelation.

The Apostle Paul discussed these same concepts in his letter to the Corinthians.

> *For I determined not to know any thing among you, save Jesus Christ, and him crucified.*
>
> [1 CORINTHIANS 2:2]

The only ministry that the sinner is able to receive from the Holy Spirit is the message of Christ crucified. When he believes this, he crosses over from spiritual death and receives eternal life, the very nature of God. This translates him out of darkness.

Natural man

But the natural man receiveth not the things of the Spirit of God: for they are foolishness unto him: neither can he know them, because they are spiritually discerned.

[1 CORINTHIANS 2:14]

The term "natural man" implies that there is more than one category of humanity. This term refers to the man who is dead in sins and locked up under spiritual death; thus a spiritual illiterate. This corresponds to the candle under the bushel in Jesus' profound parable. The problem of the man who is locked under spiritual death is not that God does not want to talk to him but that much of what God says is lost to him because he does not have the spiritual capacity to receive the things of God. This natural man is unable to discern the things of God, for they are foolishness to him. It is worse than teaching a Ph.D. syllabus to a day old baby. The point here is that there is a challenge on man's side that limits him from fellowshipping with God on terms of equality. The spiritually dead spirit is unable to comprehend at the level of the reborn spirit and of God. The human spirit that is spiritually dead cannot penetrate into God's wisdom. All things remain unclear, uncertain and mysterious.

For what man knoweth the things of a man, save the spirit of man which is in him? even so the things of God knoweth no man, but the Spirit of God.

[1 CORINTHIANS 2:11]

"The things of a man" refers more specifically to a man who is dead in sins; therefore it means the things of spiritual death. A man can only know the things of his nature and if that nature is spiritual death, then his knowledge is constrained by spiritual death. The question "What man knows the things of man?" illustrates the general principle that your human spirit knows all about you. As a result, the spirit of a man locked in spiritual death knows only what spiritual death allows. In the born again experience, "we have not received the spirit of the world". The spirit of the world is the nature of spiritual death introduced unto this earth by Adam. Therefore because a Christian has the nature of God, he knows beyond the limits of spiritual death. He has received the capacity to know as God knows. The life of God is the highest form of intelligence.

In his letter to the Jews at Rome, Paul refers to this nature of spiritual death as the spirit of bondage to fear (Rom. 8:15). He is saying that man left to himself can only know spiritual death and nothing beyond that because his spirit is a prisoner of that nature of death. Spiritual death imposes a veil on the spiritual mind and drastically reduces its intelligence. The spirit of bondage refers to our former status as slaves of sin when we were not in Christ (Rom. 6:20). You see, through the new birth, God did not renovate, rebrand or improve "the spirit of bondage again to fear". We now have the status of sons and as sons we can call him Abba Father (Rom. 8:15). The New Birth is the reception of the spirit of adoption by which we cry Abba Father. This "spirit of adoption" is not the Holy Spirit; it is the death of the slave and the birth of the son.

Watch out for the capitals

Due to the capitalization of "S" in Spirit of God in the statement, "Even so the things of God knoweth no man but the Spirit of God", we assume that it refers to the Holy Spirit. That should not be the case because up till that point Paul has been discussing how spiritual death reduces the comprehension of the human spirit. He is contrasting the knowing capacity of man's spirit in spiritual death in Adam and man's spirit quickened to life in Christ. We know the meaning of the term, "Spirit of God" by observing the context in which it is written. Here, the term "Spirit of God" refers to the born again human spirit because it is a spirit and as to its origin it is "of God" since it is born of God (1 John 4:4). The things of God are the things of divine life. There is marked difference between the spiritual intellect and comprehension of man in Adam and man in Christ.

The reborn spirit of man now knows beyond the limits imposed by spiritual death because man's spirit is now born of God. The rebirth of man's spirit is the act of setting the candle on the candlestick so that it can give to man the light that it has received from God. The principle is that your nature imposes a boundary on what you are capable of knowing. The sinner does not understand God because the sinner does not have the nature with which to do so. This is why he said, "the natural man receiveth not the things of the Spirit of God … neither can he know them …" (1 Cor. 12:14). It is not that he does not want to. He cannot know them. We each receive a new spirit from God at the new birth so that we can be taught of God about the things of God. Man is only able to know God because man has now received the spirit, which is of God. The subject has not changed; this "spirit which is of God" is not the Holy Ghost but the reborn spirit. It is not a change in the Holy Ghost that causes us to know God but the change is within our spirits when we receive the new nature. When we make these various terms refer to the Holy Spirit rather than the recreated human spirit, we rob ourselves of the opportunity to appreciate what the Lord Jesus has accomplished in the New Birth.

> *Now we have received, not the spirit of the world, but the spirit which is of God; that we might know the things that are freely given to us of God.*
>
> [1 CORINTHIANS 2:12]

When did we receive?

We received in the New Birth.

What have we received in the New Birth?

We have received the spirit, which is of God. This is the reborn human spirit.

Why have we received the spirit, which is of God?

We have received the spirit, which is of God, in order that we might know.

Man in spiritual death already knew the unedifying things of darkness. This additional "knowing" that we now have, as a result of receiving the spirit of God, is a new and higher kind of knowledge. The implication is that there are myriads of important facts over and above our former circumference of knowledge.

What are we to know?

We are to know the things that have been freely given to us by God because our spiritual nature has changed.

These were the things that ears had not heard or eyes seen but yet God had planned for our glory (1 Cor. 2:9). The reason for that statement, "eyes have not seen nor ears heard" was not because God was withholding anything from man but that the spiritual sense of seeing and hearing was veiled by spiritual death. The spiritually dead man is both blind and deaf to God but alive to evil. The New Birth gives to us spiritual senses that hear God and see into the divine things clearly. When we receive the life and nature of God in Christ Jesus, our human spirit receives the capacity to see and hear the very things that had been hid since the foundation of the world unto our glory (1 Cor. 2:7).

In 1 Corinthians 2, Paul is showing that the change that happens within man's spirit to recreate him and translate him out of darkness is not simply a form of fire insurance that delivers him from the Lake of Fire; it is the reception of intelligence as it exists in the heart of God.

As a believer, your recreated human spirit possesses the intimate knowledge of God who is truth; it has the light of God. Therefore when you stand in the presence of deception, your light bulb will let you know that what is being communicated is contrary to truth. If you learn how to listen to this new nature, you experience deliverance from lies and manipulation.

Spiritually discerned

But the natural man receiveth not the things of the Spirit of God: for they are foolishness unto him: neither can he know them, because they are spiritually discerned.

[1 CORINTHIANS 2:14]

The Word of God is a discerner of the thoughts and intents of the heart; therefore, there is a measure of discerning that comes through fellowshipping with God's Word. We also discern with our spirits. This is supernatural comprehension by the reborn spirit as the Holy Spirit teaches it. It is personalized instruction from God's Spirit into our lives. You notice that good teachers of the Word try to use analogies and illustrations to get their points across. They are looking for those aids that will help seal the truth into our understanding but since they are talking to a crowd, they have to use ideas that appeal to the majority but then there are specifics that will help you. Such personalized applications are not between you and the ministers who are addressing the crowd but between your spirit and the Holy Ghost. The Holy Ghost as the Teacher of your new nature delivers a personalized service to you by giving you exact illustrations that help you get a bible truth at your level of maturity.

The teacher of our new nature

I have yet many things to say unto you, but ye cannot bear them now. Howbeit when he, the Spirit of truth, is come, he will guide you into all truth: for he shall not speak of himself; but whatsoever he shall hear, that shall he speak: and he will shew you things to come.

[JOHN 16:12-13]

Jesus was speaking spiritual things but the disciples were natural men whose main tool for receiving spiritual things was a grossly inadequate brain. There was a great mismatch. Jesus had gone about as far as spirit-to-brain conversation could permit. Peter and the disciples did not understand the majority of what Jesus said. If you try to use your brain to grasp what the Holy Spirit is teaching you, you immediately and drastically reduce what can be conveyed to you. You'd find that your brain would require the Holy Spirit to go below kindergarten speed in order that the brain will not be overloaded. This is what Jesus meant when He told Peter, "you cannot bear it". Peter had the spirit of the world in him at that point in time. It was not that Peter was unwilling; it was not a function of willingness but of ability. At that point, Peter did not have the spiritual capacity to handle the things the Jesus had to say. Peter at this point was an authentic specimen of spiritual death. Until he received a new nature, he did not have the capacity to bear spiritual truth of the sort that Jesus wanted to communicate to him. The speed and depth of comprehension of the recreated spirit is way more advanced than that of the soul.

The Holy Ghost is our Teacher who is given to us by the Father to show us what is already freely ours in Christ Jesus (John 16:15); and just like all teachers, He can only teach a syllabus that the student can assimilate. In order to be taught of God and know God precisely, we had to first receive a recreated spirit that is born into the family of love. We can now bear the things that Jesus has to say to us by the Holy Ghost who takes the things of Jesus and gives them to us. The Holy Ghost can only give the things of Jesus to those who have the nature and life of Jesus. This is comparing spiritual things to spiritual.

But we speak the wisdom of God in a mystery, even the hidden wisdom, which God ordained before the world unto our glory:
[1 CORINTHIANS 2:7]

The wisdom of God was always available in God but was hidden from the standpoint of the man, who is enslaved by spiritual death. Man in spiritual death was in darkness; he was outside the domain of God's life and light therefore those things were hidden from his view. What

Paul is saying is that since we have received eternal life, the nature of God, we are no longer under the dominion of death; therefore, the wisdom that was previously hidden is now no longer hidden. He could now tap into the deep things of God that God intended for the glory of all those who receive His life and nature. God's wisdom is fully exposed to the one who possesses eternal life.

Searching the deep things of God

But God hath revealed them unto us by his Spirit: for the Spirit searcheth all things, yea, the deep things of God.

[1 CORINTHIANS 2:10]

The capitalization of Spirit leads us to believe that he is referring to the Holy Spirit. I hope it is obvious to the reader that God the Father does not search Himself. Why would the Holy Spirit who is as much God as the Father is, need to search the depths of God since he is God? The depths of the Father are also the depths of the Holy Spirit as well as the depths of God the Son. These are all co-equal and one. They do not search one another.

The spirit that is searching the deep things of God is the human spirit who has been freed from the constraints of spiritual death and has now received the capacity to fellowship with the Father on terms of equality through the gift of righteousness.

Solomon has some beautiful insights on this capacity of the reborn spirit to search the depths of God.

The spirit of man is the candle of the LORD, searching all the inward parts of the belly.

[PROVERBS 20:27]

Jesus referring to our spirits said, "out of your bellies shall flow rivers" (John 7:38). The belly refers to the human spirit. Solomon was given insight into the day of the rebirth of the human spirit in what we now know as the born again experience. That experience was not available in Solomon's day because the redeemer had not yet come. God revealed to Solomon that the human spirit is the candle of the Lord. Candles need light in order to project them on our path. Since the human spirit is God's candle, God is the only One that can light your candle. In the New Birth, God lit your candle (Prov. 18:28). The nature of God, which is life and light, will be used to light the candle of man's spirit. Your candle now has divine light from God's life (John 1:4). Your recreated spirit has been equipped with God's life as light to search out the strategies of God. This provides the foundation for God to fellowship with our spirits and to use our spirits to search all the inward parts of our bellies. God uses our spirits to teach us all that we need to know.

God will communicate all truth to you by teaching your spirit all things. You have a nature within your spirit that God Himself will use to search out all the wisdom that you need. There is tremendous search capacity built into your spirit by God. The human spirit is a spiritual search engine that taps into the eternal dimension of God.

We believers are the ones who through our reborn spirits search the depths of God. We can now comprehend God the same way one giraffe comprehends another giraffe but the rabbit does not, for rabbits and giraffes are not the same species.

How do we participate in this wisdom? Paul gives us further instruction.

> *Which things also we speak, not in the words which man's wisdom teacheth, but which the Holy Ghost teacheth; comparing spiritual things with spiritual.*
>
> ### [1 CORINTHIANS 2:13]

A man ruled by spiritual death is not treated as spiritual even though he is a spirit being. He is classified as a natural man because the only things that are real to him are of the senses. The Holy Ghost does not compare spiritual with natural. He can only compare spiritual with spiritual. The Holy Ghost cannot compare His own spiritual with anything in the natural man because man outside Christ did not have an equivalent nature with which the Holy Ghost could teach man. What man had was spiritual death. You cannot compare spiritual death with the life and nature of God. Once we were recreated in our spirits with God's nature, we are now spiritual. The Holy Ghost now has something within man's spiritual nature that He can compare with His own spiritual nature. This is another way of saying that the things of God are understood spiritually through the reborn spirit because as He is, so are we.

Comparison implies some sort of commonality between different things. The life of God is the commonality between God's Spirit and your reborn spirit. This forms the basis of the comparison. Both God and believers are spirit beings in the same family. It is now possible to compare or exchange things between the two. The Holy Spirit helps us compare what is within us with what is within Christ in us. Through this searching process, we are tapping into the wisdom and strategies of God.

The secret behind the secrets

Paul taught spiritual secrets. Thankfully, he does not just give us these secrets; he lets us into the secret behind the secrets that he taught by showing us the source of the revelations that he brilliantly presented to the church. Paul's reborn spirit obtained what used to be hidden wisdom, for the benefit of the church. He then explains in 1 Corinthians 2 that we can understand the things, he is communicating to us in his letters because we are of the same ilk, products of the same womb and partakers of the same life and new nature. No one has a better or superior New Birth than another. Our new nature contains the apparatus for grasping the depths of that revelation. It is because we possess this new nature that we are now speaking freely of the things spiritual death once hid from us.

We release divine wisdom by speaking. We do not speak this in a language that man's wisdom teaches. The Holy Ghost first taught Paul through a language that He supplied to Paul. This language did not flow from man's brain. Whatever Paul was saying through that language was actually Holy Spirit-taught words. Through this Spirit-taught language, wisdom was communicated to him beyond what his biological senses of seeing and hearing ever conveyed. It was through the words of this language that he received new light and fresh insight beyond what he knew when he was a Pharisee bound under spiritual death. This Holy Spirit-supplied language is none other than the spiritual language that we know as other tongues. The supernatural language of tongues was the means through which the Holy Spirit edified Paul to know the wisdom that was previously hidden in God. Paul exercised himself extensively through this means of spiritual edification until he wrote out whole epistles that he was then teaching to the Churches. God is teaching us today to also learn to speak out divine wisdom in words that the Holy Ghost teaches us.

There are a few expressions that we should understand in relation to all this.

Spirit of His Son

And because ye are sons, God hath sent forth the Spirit of his Son into your hearts, crying, Abba, Father.

[GALATIANS 4:6]

What is meant by, "God has sent the Spirit of his Son"? He means that the same nature of sonship that made the resurrected Lord a son is the same nature within the spirit of the believer that makes the believer a son also. On the scale of sonship, you weigh the same as Jesus. He means that the Lord Jesus is not more of a son than you are to the Father. We have the Spirit of Christ.

The spiritual equivalent is saying that as sinners we used to have the spirit of Adam, which is the spirit of the world. This does not mean that we had Adam's human spirit, for Adam has his own human spirit and we each have ours. Possessing the spirit of Adam or the spirit of the world simply means we were partakers of spiritual death that entered the human race through Adam as the head of the family. In the same vein having the spirit of Christ does not mean that we have the human spirit of the Lord Jesus, for no human can have the human spirit of another man. The Spirit of Christ is the nature that made Jesus a son by resurrection. To have the spirit of Christ means that because of our union with Christ in resurrection, we are what He is as a son. The overcoming life that is in Christ is now in the believing one.

The mind of Christ

For who hath known the mind of the Lord, that he may instruct him? but we have the mind of Christ.
[1 CORINTHIANS 2:16]

The mind of Christ does not mean the personal brain of the Lord Jesus. There is a mind that goes with the nature that makes us sons. The mind of Christ is the intelligence that emanates from the "spirit of his son". It is called the mind of Christ because the Lord Jesus is the Author of it. Therefore, to say that the believer has the mind of Christ is another way of saying that the believer's spirit possesses the intelligence faculty that goes along with possessing the same nature as Christ. It is the intelligence and wisdom of the hidden man of the heart. The spirit of the believer has a spiritual mind, with which it comprehends spiritual things because he has exactly the same nature as the Lord Jesus Christ.

Comprehending through the mind of Christ

As a new creation, the Holy Ghost helps us primarily by transferring into our spiritual mind, the exact contents of the mind of the Lord. This is because the capacity of your spiritual mind is same as that of the Lord Jesus. It is not through the brain but through this spiritual mind that we grasp the plans of God. The born again man has the mind of Christ which causes his spiritual eyes and ears to see and hear the plans of God – major on that! You are to dare to believe that you have an anointing from the Holy One by which you know all things (1 John 2:20). Your spirit is more intelligent than your brain and will pick up facts that your brain cannot substantiate at the moment. Do not ignore these knowings.

A language that the Holy Ghost teacheth

Which things also we speak, not in the words which man's wisdom teacheth, but which the Holy Ghost teacheth; comparing spiritual things with spiritual.

[1 CORINTHIANS 2:13]

The Holy Ghost is the Teacher who trains our new nature in comparing spiritual things. When Paul mentions the third member of the Godhead, he calls him by name – the Holy Ghost. He does not say the Spirit of God because that term is open to interpretation depending on what the verse is referring to. There is a language that the Holy Ghost teaches. This supernatural language compares the deep things of God's life with the things of our new nature. This language is not from our brain cells, from our culture or natural reasoning but from the intelligence of God within the spiritual DNA of the new nature in Christ. Our spirit maintains correspondence with God's Spirit (Rom. 8:16).

The supernatural language communicated by the Holy Spirit causes us to know the mind of the spirit. You come to understand many things that you don't know how you know them but you know that you know them. This is the spiritual mind at work.

We are extracting that wisdom which is no longer hidden to us. It is really up to us to use the language that the Holy Ghost generates within our spiritual minds to lift us above the deception of the flesh and the senses, until He separates us from following human traditions unto the things that God intended for your glory. When we speak in tongues, the Holy Spirit is teaching us.

When we pray out in other tongues, which is the language the Holy Spirit teaches our spirit, the mysteries spoken out are not the traditions of men but God teaching us spiritual things. The Holy Ghost as the Teacher of our new nature helps us by taking those mysteries that we have spoken out to build out a syllabus for training us. This is the training that equips the spiritual one to judge all things from the mind of Christ.

Though the Christians at Corinth had received the capacity to understand the secrets of God in the New Birth, Paul could not convey much to them. This was because they had experienced divisions. These divisions do not so much refer to strife and quarrels in the church. People focus on those things but strife and quarrels are the symptom and not the real issue. The divisions refer to the Corinthians separating themselves from following the mind of Christ. The mind of Christ will never lead you into strife but the traditions of men will. Division is prioritizing carnal reasoning above the mind of Christ.

Switching from the carnal mind

For to be carnally minded is death; but to be spiritually minded is life and peace.

[ROMANS 8:6]

The carnal mind is the darkened and grossly limited understanding produced by spiritual death (Eph. 4:18). This mind does not function in the life of God and does not subject itself to God's nature. The carnal mind is the greatest limitation that your spirit faces on the earth. The carnal mind is like gravity that pulls us towards death but the mind of the spirit causes us to escape from the limitations of the carnal mind and brings us to a place of certainty and knowing.

Praying with understanding

What is it then? I will pray with the spirit, and I will pray with the understanding also: I will sing with the spirit, and I will sing with the understanding also.

[1 CORINTHIANS 14:15]

I used to think praying with understanding just referred to the prayers I pray with a language that is known to my mind. Actually, praying with understanding is more powerful than that; it refers to praying with our understanding of the Word of God. It is scriptural to pray with our understanding of the Word of God that we already know. The Word of God is the vocabulary of prayer (John 15:7). If we are not praying the Word of God but just blurting out whatever comes to our natural mind, we are not praying. Prayer is the Word flowing out of your lips to God. His analysis was that the primary way for a Christian to pray is to pray in tongues. Praying in understanding is second best to praying in tongues. This is why he saw praying in understanding as "also".

Likewise the Spirit also helpeth our infirmities: for we know not what we should pray for as we ought: but the Spirit itself maketh intercession for us with groanings which cannot be uttered. And he that searcheth the hearts knoweth what is the mind of the Spirit, because he maketh intercession for the saints according to the will of God.

[ROMANS 8:26]

The greatest infirmity of the unbeliever is the darkness projected by their spirits upon their understanding (Eph. 4:18). For the born again man, the spirit is not the limitation, for our spirits are now complete in Christ Jesus (Col. 2:10). The infirmity of the believer is the infirmity of not knowing – it is a soul that has not learnt to be a servant of the recreated spirit. While we know how to pray, we often find our soul stumped because it does not know what to pray. This is because we are more conscious of the carnal mind than we are of the mind of Christ, which knows the will of God for that situation.

When he says, "Likewise the Spirit helpeth", he is referring to the Holy Spirit coming to our aid. That word helpeth is a Greek word that means cooperating together against a weight or taking hold together with us against a weight. The Holy Ghost is not our first help in relation to our infirmities for the Holy Ghost helps likewise. Likewise as what you may ask? 'Likewise' as the first help that God gave us, when we were without strength (Rom. 5:6). The reborn spirit is God's first help to the believer. The Word is not your help until you know it. It is the Word of God that we know that helps us against the infirmity of ignorance. So we have a three-fold help – the recreated spirit, the Word of God that we know and the Holy Ghost.

God's Word is always adequate enough for any situation but there are times when your knowledge of the Word of God is not adequate for a situation. There is no deficiency in the Word but in our knowledge of it.

The help of the Holy Ghost is given to us in the form of utterance, which we then need to choose to voice out. Our prayers are not authorized for action from heaven, until the prayer is literally spoken out of one's mouth. No matter how dark things look, the answer must flow out of our mouths. We must not leave things in the thought realm only. In Genesis, "the Spirit of God moved upon the face of the waters" (Gen. 1:2). This all-knowing Holy Spirit knew that the Father wanted light but the Spirit of God did not move until He heard God say, "let there be light."

When your back is against the wall, instead of griping and complaining, act on the word that you know and then go beyond what you know by praying in tongues until your understanding is enriched. Those prayers that we pray in tongues are also meant to be answered. The Holy Spirit helps us by teaching us from that place of not knowing to a place where we know. He supplies this help in form of utterances because the supernatural language that the Holy Spirit instructs us with is our access into the mind of Christ. This is why when we yield to the utterance of the Holy Ghost, we trigger that sense of knowing.

This supernatural language causes us to know the mind of the spirit, which merges with our mind as we flow in the supernatural language. The intention of God is to cause us to exchange functioning by the carnal mind with functioning by the mind of the spirit.

As we continue to speak in the supernatural language, we give the Holy Spirit the raw materials to use to help us to prioritize the mind of the spirit above the carnal mind.

God wants us to pray beyond our limitations; especially the limitations of knowledge. Many times, when we think of the manifestation of the sons of God, some think that these will be products of some revival in the last days but the truth is that it is not stated anywhere in the bible that an end time revival will change the church. If anything, it is saints that release revival because they have submitted themselves to the fundamentals of submitting to God in prayer and praying in the spirit.

Mixing confession of the Word with the language

Do we get the value that we would have gotten from confession of the Word from just praying in tongues?

When we meditate on the Word of God, we wear down the un-renewed mind, which functions as the unjust judge of our soul. The un-renewed mind stirs up war against our reborn spirit. It imposes a limit on the outflow of spiritual things from the human spirit for the soul functions like a joint.

Our soul is not like our spirit and does not believe the things that our spirit already accepts to be true. Therefore, our soul gives our spirit a lot of trouble. Your soul needs an education to free it from spiritual illiteracy. The way the soul is designed, whatever information you have in abundance is the one that your soul will be most convinced about, even if the conviction is not in line with the truth of God's Word. The soul therefore passes flakey judgment in important matters of life. The judge considers the evidence set before him, whether the evidence is moral or immoral. The unjust judge does not operate in the grace of God but within the framework of condemnation, fear and anxiety; which choke out the experience of God's mercy in our lives. We use the confession of the Word of God to train the soul out of being an unjust judge and help it on the journey to judging righteous judgment in line with the Word.

We use the confession of our mouths to overdose on the Word till the unjust judge of the mind starts delivering righteous judgment. When things in the natural world bombard you with facts, hold fast to God's Word and remember that the Word of God is the highest fact that can change your mind. When we pray in tongues, we are setting the edification process in motion (1 Cor. 14:4). We are like students submitting ourselves to the professor in a lecture room. This is what accelerates the opening of the door of revelation knowledge.

6

Tongues in the Book of Acts

And they were all filled with the Holy Ghost, and began to speak with other tongues, as the Spirit gave them utterance.

[ACTS 2:4]

Jesus had said to His disciples before His ascension to heaven, "Tarry ye in the city of Jerusalem, until ye be endued with power from on high" (Lk. 24:49). This enduing with power was what culminated in speaking with tongues in Acts 2. The disciples faithfully waited in Jerusalem for this to happen. There were others in the book of Acts, who received the Holy Ghost with the evidence of speaking in tongues but interestingly these did not happen in Jerusalem! The instruction that the Lord Jesus gave His disciples to wait in Jerusalem was a pre-requisite for them but not for any other group. This was why that instruction was never repeated in the whole New Testament.

It was a specific instruction for that group.

> *Therefore being by the right hand of God exalted, and having received of the Father the promise of the Holy Ghost, he hath shed forth this, which ye now see and hear.*
>
> [ACTS 2:33]

When Peter said that Jesus shed forth "This which you now see and hear", he could have been referring to the inspired preaching he delivered on that day, after he had first spoken in tongues. It might also have been referring to the speaking in tongues itself or both.

Now that Jesus was seated in the heavens at God's right hand, His position was in the heavenlies but His ministry was still needed on the earth. It was a new dispensation in which His new ministry could only be carried out by a new outpouring of the Holy Ghost. Without this outpouring, the disciples could not carry on with the post-resurrection ministry of Jesus on the earth.

The event in Acts 2 marked the first outpouring of the Spirit. They were tarrying in Jerusalem for the first outpouring. All they could do was tarry. The outpoured Spirit was a part of Jesus' ministry from heaven and it shows that obtaining our salvation was not the last thing Jesus did in heaven. Men responded to that outpouring by speaking in tongues. This was the first instance of the gift of tongues ever occurring on the earth.

Peter quotes Joel's prophecy as scriptural backing for what transpired at Pentecost. Peter knew about Joel's prophecy prior to the day of Pentecost, just as every devout Jew did but he now had a revelation from the Holy Ghost as to its true meaning. We must find scriptural foundation for our spiritual experiences. We are to let the Word birth our spiritual experiences. If there is no Word for it, you are on shaky foundations.

Is tongues for evangelising foreign lands?

The disciples who gathered on the day of Pentecost were filled with the Holy Ghost and spoke in tongues. Following that, we are told that 3,000 people received salvation on that day alone! God had lit their candle. On the back of this, some people conclude that speaking in tongues was given so that believers will use it to evangelise foreign nations where there are language barriers.

There is no disputing that 3,000 Jews received eternal life that day but how did this come about?

Did those 3,000 say, "We do hear in our own tongue how Jehovah sent His son to destroy the works of darkness, take our sin upon Himself, and get crucified to die our death in order to destroy the dominion of spiritual death over us. We also heard how He rose up the third day and presented His blood in the holy place in heaven as proof of an everlasting covenant. We hear that we are to believe in this Son and by believing, receive eternal life"?

If that was what they had heard, then it is true that through speaking in tongues, the gospel has been preached to these devout Jews but that was not what they heard. I just made up that quote above.

These Jews who had come from every known part of the world heard something for they said,

> *Cretes and Arabians, we do hear them speak in our tongues the wonderful works of God.*

[ACTS 2.11]

What did they hear?

The exact content of the wonderful works that those devout Jews heard is shrouded in mystery. The bible does not tell us the exact wording. We do however know that whatever they heard it did not make the hearers ask questions like "Brethren, what must we do to be saved?"

After the Jews heard the wonderful works of God as a result of the 120 believers' speaking in tongues, Peter still had to get up and preach the gospel to them. Therefore, when the bible says that they heard the disciples speaking the wonderful works of God, what they heard was praise. The people heard praise initially when the believers were speaking in tongues. They did not hear evangelical preaching.

> But Peter, standing up with the eleven, lifted up his voice, and said unto them, Ye men of Judaea, and all ye that dwell at Jerusalem, be this known unto you, and hearken to my words: Now when they heard this, they were pricked in their heart, and said unto Peter and to the rest of the apostles, Men and brethren, what shall we do? Then Peter said unto them, Repent, and be baptized every one of you in the name of Jesus Christ for the remission of sins, and ye shall receive the gift of the Holy Ghost.
>
> [ACTS 2:11, 37-38]

Peter preached on the day of Pentecost but he did not do it in tongues. Speaking in tongues got everyone's attention and when they had a firm hold of everyone's attention, Peter stood up to preach. My guess is that he preached his sermon in a language common to all the Jews that were gathered. This would naturally be Hebrew, Aramaic or some other commonly understood language. This much was obvious though - it was not tongues. In order to preach effectively, your hearers have to understand what you are saying.

What did Peter say when he preached?

That bit was recorded. He preached the gospel. He freely discussed the true meaning of the Psalms of David and used it to preach about the death and resurrection of Jesus! Speaking in tongues before preaching opened him up to the truths of God's Word. Scriptures that he had read as a young man now flooded his heart with meaning. His understanding was now fruitful.

> Therefore let all the house of Israel know assuredly, that God hath

made the same Jesus, whom ye have crucified, both Lord and Christ.
Now when they heard this, they were pricked in their heart, and said
unto Peter and to the rest of the apostles, Men and brethren, what shall
we do?

[ACTS 2:36-37]

What was the effect on the hearers?

They were pricked in their hearts. They asked, "What must we do"?

Peter's message did not just stir the people's emotions. It pricked their hearts. We are not told that their hearts were pricked when the disciples spoke in tongues.

Proper preaching of the gospel is a two-way street. At first, Peter preached to the people and in response to his preaching, the people asked him questions. Peter then provided answers to their questions, until they made a choice to accept or reject the offer of salvation. How would you hold this conversation with the unbeliever in tongues? For all you know, if you attempt to preach the gospel in tongues, you might have spoken to the people about the exploits of Samson in defeating the Philistines!

While the idea of going into any foreign land and preaching powerfully about the things of Christ in their native tongue through tongues sounds wonderful, we don't have a bible account of it. Preaching in a language known to the hearer is the pattern that we see in Acts, as well as throughout the bible. Speaking in tongues is not designed as a gift for preaching the gospel to the unsaved. While that is not impossible, if it were to happen, it would be a supernatural sign.

The 120 that spoke in tongues that day clearly did not speak supposing that they were preaching the gospel. When they felt it was time to preach, one of them stood up to deliver the sermon.

Paul also gives a clue along these lines. When referring to teaching believers he said, "Yet in the church I had rather speak five words with my understanding, that by my voice I might teach others also, than ten thousand words in an unknown tongue" (1 Cor. 14:19). The primary purpose of tongues is not for teaching or preaching, to believers or unbelievers.

When the people heard the gospel they had questions. When people have questions, we should not waive them away as unimportant – we should supply answers. These days, after preaching we immediately request that people make a decision but this was not Peter's style. He anticipated, entertained and answered their questions. Peter did not immediately ask for a show of hands after his sermons or for people to fill decision cards. Our evangelistic sermons today are not designed to cause the hearers to ask questions. When tongue-talking, spirit-filled people minister, there ought to be questions in the people's hearts.

People have a mind. It is because of the barrier imposed by the soul that people don't just automatically get born again once they hear the gospel (2 Cor. 4:4). If not for the soul component of men, you could effectively go to the most crowded places, amplify the Word on loud speakers and every single person who hears it would just get born again. Thankfully, that's not the way it works. Otherwise, someone could broadcast evil over the airwaves and we'd all just act out the evil automatically.

When the people said, "what must we do?", Peter could not just respond, "I have already preached God's eternal word, now accept salvation and stop asking questions". The folks had questions. Spirit inspired preaching should make people think. It should lead people to ask good questions.

The absence of good questions reflects badly on the typical church service today. This question-and-answer format is the best format for effective preaching to the unsaved.

And the Spirit bade me go with them, nothing doubting. Moreover these six brethren accompanied me, and we entered into the man's house:

[ACTS 11:12]

We have more evidence from the book of Acts that the primal purpose of tongues is not evangelical in nature. Concerning those in Cornelius' house, Peter says, "God gave them the like gift as he did unto us, who believed on the Lord Jesus Christ;" (Acts 11:17). We know that God was definitely not preaching salvation to the Jewish Christians since Peter and the six brethren that went with him were already Christians. Why would you preach salvation to those who were already born again? That would be like taking sand to the desert! The Jewish Christians that came with Peter were already born again; if anything, it was the Gentiles who needed to receive the gift of salvation. The Jewish Christians present, heard these Gentiles speak in tongues and magnify God. What happened through the tongues was not evangelistic but the worship of God.

Since Peter was part of the crew that got filled with the Spirit in Acts 2, his witness has to count for something. According to him, those on whom the Holy Ghost fell in Cornelius' house received "the like gift" as Peter did in Acts 2. This would mean that what happened in Acts 2 was similar to what happened in Cornelius' house. Since the purpose was not evangelistic in Cornelius' house, it cannot be evangelistic in Acts 2!

The evangelistic dimension to Acts 2 was through Peter's preaching and not through speaking in tongues.

The typical purpose for speaking in tongues is for God to be magnified in the heart and mind of the Christian, thus enriching and edifying the Christian supernaturally. Speaking in tongues is given by God to the believer, so that the believer can commune with God as he magnifies God and speaks divine secrets. The primary purpose of tongues is devotional and not evangelistic.

Luke's silence concerning the three thousand

> *Then Peter said unto them, Repent, and be baptized every one of you in the name of Jesus Christ for the remission of sins, and ye shall receive the gift of the Holy Ghost. For the promise is unto you, and to your children, and to all that are afar off, even as many as the LORD our God shall call. And with many other words did he testify and exhort, saying, Save yourselves from this untoward generation. Then they that gladly received his word were baptized: and the same day there were added unto them about three thousand souls.42 And they continued stedfastly in the apostles' doctrine and fellowship, and in breaking of bread, and in prayers.*
>
> [ACTS 2:38-41]

Peter had told them that the Lord Jesus "has poured out what you now see and hear". So we know they saw some things and they heard other things. They might have seen the tongues of fire that rested on the disciples as well as heard the sound of a rushing mighty wind but we definitely know that they all heard the disciples speak in other tongues "because each one heard them speaking in his own language" Acts 2:6.

Under the inspiration of the Holy Ghost, Peter said that if all three thousand repented and were baptised in the name of Jesus, they would receive the promise of the Father. Their repentance means that they became Christians and their water baptism witnessed publicly to the Jews who were present that their sins had been forgiven. They fulfilled the conditions set by Peter; therefore Luke leaves us to conclude that they also received the promise of the Father. This promise of the Father did not refer to getting born again but to being filled with the Spirit. The inescapable conclusion is that all three thousand received the promise of the Father and were filled with the Holy Ghost as a result. It would be normal for them to expect to also speak in tongues as confirmation that they had received the promise of the Father. I admit that Luke fails to say in direct terms, if the three thousand spoke in tongues. His failure to state so, does not prove that they did not speak in tongues. Why does Luke not make a point of always stating if new believers spoke in tongues or not? I believe that this is because his primal aim is to show that salvation was received whenever men believed the gospel and he went about demonstrating the evidences of salvation. Well, how can we be sure that they spoke with tongues?

Instances where people spoke in tongues

Now, let us see what more we can learn from the events of the day of Pentecost.

> *And when the day of Pentecost was fully come, they were all with one accord in one place. And suddenly there came a sound from heaven as of a rushing mighty wind, and it filled all the house where they were sitting. And there appeared unto them cloven tongues like as of fire, and it sat upon each of them. And they were all filled with the Holy Ghost, and began to speak with other tongues, as the Spirit gave them utterance.*

[ACTS 2;1-4]

The principle of first mention is a principle of interpreting scripture that says that the first occurrence of a subject in scripture establishes an unchangeable pattern that helps fix its meaning. Things start out at first in very simple form and then progressively get more complex.

Based on this principle, we can learn a lot from the operation of tongues by examining the very first record of believers actually speaking in tongues.

Paul explains that, "if thou shalt confess with thy mouth the Lord Jesus, and shalt believe in thine heart that God hath raised him from the dead, thou shalt be saved" (Rom. 10:9). Based on that principle, when "Thomas answered and said unto him, My Lord and my God" John 20:28, Thomas became a Christian. Therefore by the time we get to Acts 2, Thomas was a Christian. The principle therefore is that only those who are born again can be filled with the Holy Ghost (Acts

11:17). Prior to Acts 2, the disciples were saved but not filled with the Spirit, thus it is possible to be born again but not filled with the Holy Ghost. Being born again is not the same thing as being filled with the Spirit.

We find that when the believers were filled with the Holy Ghost for the first time, they immediately followed it with a particular action – they began to speak with other tongues. This fact that it is the believer who starts to speak in tongues is an important one to understand. It means that we always retain the ability to override the prompting of the Holy Ghost when He inspires us to speak in tongues. The fact that many believers successfully continue to override the Holy Spirit's promptings is why many never really speak in tongues to start with and it is why those who speak in tongues do not progress much further in spiritual things.

This is that

For these are not drunken, as ye suppose, seeing it is but the third hour of the day. But this is that which was spoken by the prophet Joel; And it shall come to pass in the last days, saith God, I will pour out of my Spirit upon all flesh: and your sons and your daughters shall prophesy, and your young men shall see visions, and your old men shall dream dreams: And on my servants and on my handmaidens I will pour out in those days of my Spirit; and they shall prophesy:

[ACTS 2:15-18]

Peter said that the scriptural explanation of the disciples' speaking in tongues at Pentecost was Joel's prophecy concerning the last days. While Joel's prophecy did not say anything directly about speaking with tongues, it talks about young men seeing visions, old men dreaming dreams and the young ones prophesying.

Joel's prophesy therefore really means that as people yield to the Holy Spirit and start speaking in tongues; this would open the door for further manifestations of the Spirit in their lives. We should therefore expect more operations of the Spirit as soon as we start speaking in tongues. Speaking in tongues is the door into the spiritual theatre of the Spirit. We must all go past that door into more of what the Holy Spirit wants to guide us into. As you speak in tongues your dreams, visions and prophecies take on a more supernatural edge to them. So at Pentecost, we find that when believers were filled with the Holy Ghost, they responded by speaking in tongues, which should then lead them into further spiritual things.

What happened at Samaria?

Now when the apostles which were at Jerusalem heard that Samaria had received the word of God, they sent unto them Peter and John:Who, when they were come down, prayed for them, that they might receive the Holy Ghost: (For as yet he was fallen upon none of them: only they were baptized in the name of the Lord Jesus.) Then laid they their hands on them, and they received the Holy Ghost.

[ACTS 8:14-17]

In Samaria, Peter and John prayed for the new believers that they might receive the Holy Ghost. Peter and John did not tell the believers in Samaria to come over to Jerusalem in order to tarry until they be endued with power from on high as Peter and John had done many years earlier. Since the Holy Ghost is already given, they planned to get them to receive. People usually tend to receive what they believe for. Those that believe in tarrying tend to tarry a lot. While those who expect to receive end up receiving. We should tarry after we are filled and not in order to get filled.

Peter and John were to lay hands on the Samaritan believers, as a result of which these new believers were then to receive the Holy Ghost. There is an inspired little comment in that passage that the Holy Ghost was yet to fall on them. When the Holy Ghost falls on people, what are the evidences? Peter and John could instantly tell as soon as they had laid hands on the believers that they immediately received the Holy Ghost. How could anyone present tell that these disciples had received the Holy Ghost?

> *And there was great joy in that city. And when Simon saw that through*
> *laying on of the apostles' hands the Holy Ghost was given, he offered*
> *them money,*
>
> [ACTS 8:8, 18]

As a result of Phillip's ministry in Samaria, prior to the coming of
Peter and John, there was great joy in the city of Samaria. It was
not just joy but great joy. This great joy is the joy of salvation. This
confirms that the people who were going to receive the Holy Ghost
were already Christians. Simon the sorcerer must have noticed this
great joy but he did not approach Phillip to confer on him the power
to impart this great joy onto people.

When the bible says, "And when Simon saw that through laying on of
the apostles' hands the Holy Ghost was given", we know this was not
a spiritual vision. Simon was a new Christian who was still being ruled
by his senses. Simon saw with his physical senses and whatever Simon
saw convinced him that something was received because it had been
given through the laying on of hands. There was evidence just as on
the day of Pentecost.

The Laying on of hands is a means of giving the Holy Ghost and
once the Holy Ghost is given, the onus lies with the one on who
hands were laid to receive. What was it that Simon saw that caused
him to offer money?

> *Thou hast neither part nor lot in this matter: for thy heart is not right*
> *in the sight of God.*
>
> [ACTS 8:21]

Those that read this passage and concluded that Luke did not directly
say that the saints at Samaria spoke with tongues have a point if they
read it only in English. We have a strong hint as to what it was that
Simon saw because in Peter's rebuke of Simon, he said, "Thou hast

neither part nor lot in this matter …". Experts of the Greek language tell us that the Greek word translated as "matter" in that verse is better rendered as, a saying or something spoken. Therefore Peter's rebuke of Simon meant, "You have neither part nor lot in this speech or utterance"! The evidence that Simon saw was something spoken by each believer when hands were laid on them.

Furthermore, when Paul said to the Corinthians, "That in everything ye are enriched by him in all utterance" (1 Cor. 1:5), the word translated "utterance" is the very word translated as "matter" here. This would mean that utterance was imparted to the Samaritans through the laying on of hands. The Holy Spirit supplied utterance, while men cooperated by speaking out that utterance in other tongues. This agrees with the pattern in Acts 2.

Simon saw that utterance was given by the laying on of hands and received by those on whom hands were laid. What was received was not great joy. The Samaritans' corresponding action to receiving utterance was speaking in tongues. Since Peter and John were sent to minister to these new Christians as soon as they got born again, we learn that the best time to receive the Holy Spirit would be the early days of our Christian walk.

What of Ananias and Saul?

And the Lord said unto him, Arise, and go into the street which is called Straight, and enquire in the house of Judas for one called Saul, of Tarsus: for, behold, he prayeth, And hath seen in a vision a man named Ananias coming in, and putting his hand on him, that he might receive his sight. And Ananias went his way, and entered into the house; and putting his hands on him said, Brother Saul, the Lord, even Jesus, that appeared unto thee in the way as thou camest, hath sent me, that thou mightest receive thy sight, and be filled with the Holy Ghost.

[ACTS 9:11-12,17]

Saul became a Christian once he had acknowledged Jesus as Lord on the road to Damascus, during that spectacular heavenly vision. Saul was now a member of the body of Christ.

The Lord Jesus instructed Ananias to go lay hands on Saul as a fulfillment of the vision Saul had seen earlier about a man imparting restoration of vision to him by the laying on of hands. Saul was going to receive restored sight through the laying on of hands. Interestingly, when Ananias spoke to Saul, he did not just tell him that the Lord Jesus had sent him to lay hands for the restoration of Saul's sight. He says, "that thou mightiest receive thy sight, and be filled with the Holy Ghost". Thus the same Holy Ghost power that reversed Saul's blindness would also cause him to be filled with the Spirit.

When Ananias got to Saul, Saul was a baby Christian, less than a week old. Ananias did not tell the Lord, "Well Lord, you know you told us to wait in Jerusalem until we be endued with power from on high. Why then are you not instructing me to go tell Saul to tarry in Jerusalem?" Ananias did not bring it up because the command to tarry was for a specific group. Ananias was not one of those and neither was Saul. There was no need to tarry before one received the Holy Spirit.

After Ananias had ministered to Saul by the laying on of hands, the bible tells us how the scales fell from Saul's eyes but is silent on any other effect of Ananias' ministry to Saul. The Lord Jesus sent him to minister two distinct things to Saul. Did Ananias minister only the recovery of sight or was there more? Thus far, the only other two instances in the book of Acts when men received the Holy Ghost, utterance was given and they immediately responded to the utterance by speaking in tongues. Was this the case with Saul? The evidence from Paul's personal testimony when he wrote to the Corinthians is, "I thank my God, I speak with tongues more than ye all" (1 Cor. 14:18). Therefore we conclude that when Ananias laid hands on Saul, Saul did not only start seeing, he also started speaking in tongues. This is in line with the pattern in Acts 2:4.

Thus far in the book of Acts all who spoke in tongues were Jews.

Peter at Cornelius' house

While Peter yet spake these words, the Holy Ghost fell on all them which heard the word. And they of the circumcision which believed were astonished, as many as came with Peter, because that on the Gentiles also was poured out the gift of the Holy Ghost. For they heard them speak with tongues, and magnify God. Then answered Peter,

[ACTS 10:44-46]

Prior to this event, God had tried to free Peter from his religious bigotry by telling him in a trance, "What God hath cleansed, that call not thou common" (Acts 11:9). God was referring to the Gentiles. This was how God persuaded Peter to go preach to Cornelius. Peter learnt the lesson that the Gentiles were no longer unclean, therefore, the Gospel could be preached to them.

Right in the middle of Peter's preaching, the Holy Ghost fell on those who heard the preaching of God's Word. The gift of the Holy Ghost was poured out on the Gentiles.

How did Peter and his crew know that the gift of the Holy Ghost had been poured out on the Gentiles?

They could tell by what they heard the Gentiles speak out of their mouths, "for they (that's Peter and his Jewish crew) heard them (Cornelius and his Gentile crew) speak with tongues". What convinced those Jews out of their religious bigotry was when they heard the Gentiles speak with tongues. Speaking in tongues was the first great blow to the wall of division that had separated Jews from Gentiles. The Lord Jesus had personally created peace by breaking down the wall of partition that divided the Jew and Gentile. He did this by fulfilling the Law and setting it aside (Eph. 2:14); but it was speaking in tongues that caused the Jewish believers to acknowledge the reality of it!

We see that in Cornelius' house, the first Gentiles to get the outpouring of the Holy Ghost spoke in other tongues as a consequence of that outpouring. So, the terms "the Holy Ghost fell upon them", "poured out the gift of the Holy Ghost", "filled with the Spirit", "receive the Holy Ghost" are all synonymous terms. Irrespective of the term used to describe it, the response of the believer is to speak in tongues. Thus far, we can establish that the basic corresponding action to being initially filled with the spirit is to speak in other tongues. Speaking in tongues was not all there was but it is obviously the commonality, the starting point.

The Holy Spirit knew that the Jews were prejudiced but He did not refuse to fall upon the Gentiles because of prejudice on the part of the Jews. We create all sorts of rules concerning conditions under which believers can be filled with the Spirit. Thankfully, the Holy Ghost does not follow our rules!

The evidence throughout the book of Acts is that speaking in tongues is always the response of being initially filled with the spirit.

Paul at Ephesus

He said unto them, Have ye received the Holy Ghost since ye believed? And they said unto him, We have not so much as heard whether there be any Holy Ghost. Then said Paul, John verily baptized with the baptism of repentance, saying unto the people, that they should believe on him which should come after him, that is, on Christ Jesus. And when Paul had laid his hands upon them, the Holy Ghost came on them; and they spake with tongues, and prophesied.

[ACTS 19:2, 4, 6]

What we learn from this episode is that no matter how pious and genuine people are, the level of information that they have about the Holy Ghost determines if they will end up receiving the Holy Ghost. The fellows at Ephesus had not even heard if there 'be' a Holy Ghost! People that deny the Holy Spirit as well as people who are not familiar with the Holy Ghost are greatly hindered by their ignorance from receiving the gift of the Holy Ghost.

Paul's question, "Unto what then were ye baptized?" shows his shock that these folks had heard the gospel message without hearing about the Holy Ghost. This would mean that Paul typically told those he preached to about the full gospel package of salvation, for the spirit as well as the fact that they could be filled with the Holy Ghost as a result. Paul removed their ignorance by giving them knowledge, and then he laid hands on them to help them receive after which these Christians began to speak in tongues. We find that speaking in tongues quickly opened the door for another manifestation of the Spirit, the gift of prophecy. When the Holy Ghost fell on the Gentiles, they spoke with tongues and magnified God. In Ephesus, they spoke with tongues and also prophesied. Thus we find that people often receive more than just the basic tongues for edification from God, when they are initially filled with the Spirit.

The purpose of Pentecost

Let us remember that if Jesus had not resurrected after His death, He would have failed. Had He not received the gift of the Holy Ghost from the Father and then into the earth, then His sitting down at the Father's right hand would be a farce.

> *And they were all filled with the Holy Ghost, and began to speak with other tongues, as the Spirit gave them utterance.*

[ACTS 2:4]

This verse is pivotal to understanding speaking in tongues but it also showcases something larger than speaking with tongues. The disciples were filled with the Holy Ghost. They were filled with the living God just as Jesus had been full of God. Pentecost describes what happens when the Christian yields his will and submits his mouth and tongue to the indwelling Spirit of God until, not just his spirit but also his whole being is overdosed with God. Pentecost was given to man so that the ultimate purpose of redemption might be carried unfettered to its logical conclusion. The ultimate is the unleashing of God through men whose bodies had become the habitation of the living God.

It is a law of man's being that the body follows wherever the mouth leads (Jas. 3:6). Our bodies are now the laboratories, where the processes that originated in the spirit run to full completion in the body via the mouth (Prov. 13:3).

First of all, we submit our wills to the Lord. Then our wills release our mouths to speak in tongues. When the mouth is submitted to God, the whole body will follow into richer spiritual living until every substance of our being is the substance of God. It is the fullness of God. The starting place is the mouth submitted to God. God's plan though is for this to spread into every part of our physical constitution, so that the substance of God is in our mouths, fingers and eyes. People can now stare into our eyes and see God.

The life of the early church as we understand it started in tongues. It was not just that they were gathered together in one place, for if that was it, they had been gathering that way for a while. It was as they spoke in unknown tongues that they received fresh directions, organisation and power. The secret is not in copying their structures. All responded to the spirit as they spoke in other tongues and they acted in ways that helped further the plan of God for their generation.

7

Clarifying
Misconceptions

*For he that speaketh in an unknown tongue speaketh not unto men,
but unto God: for no man understandeth him; howbeit in the spirit he
speaketh mysteries.*

[1 CORINTHIANS 14:2]

The Greek word that is translated "tongues" in our English
New Testament is better translated as languages. Even today,
if someone were to ask you about your mother tongue, you
would know they are not referring to the organ of taste but to your
native language. Thus, there is really nothing mystical about tongues
if you think of it as a language, for that's what it is. It would therefore
help you, whenever you come across that word "tongues" to have
"language" at the back of your mind, so as to remove any confusion.

When "unknown" and tongues are used together, a good translation would italicize the word "unknown". This is because it was added in our English Bibles to amplify to the non-Greek speaker that the language that was spoken was not a learned one.

Let's clarify some misconceptions by adopting a question and answer format.

Question

Why are you giving importance to the subject of speaking in tongues?

It was the Lord Jesus Himself who said, "They shall speak with new tongues" (Mk. 16:17). Joel prophesied about it in Joel 2. The Prophet Isaiah wrote about it in Isaiah 28. The Lord gave instruction about it through Jude and then through the Apostle Paul, He gave us the full syllabus on this subject.

There are few spiritual themes that you find any New Testament writer dedicating a whole chapter of any New Testament book to. Paul did so for the subjects of giving, the resurrection as well as marriage. He also dedicated a whole chapter to the subject of the administration of tongues in 1 Corinthians 14. By so doing, the Lord gave this subject a prominence that we do well to remember.

On the other hand, people keep asking about this subject and bringing up all manner of arguments against its validity. We therefore find ourselves having to respond more often than not.

Question

I understand that only the original twelve Apostles can minister the infilling of the Holy Ghost. Since none of those original apostles are around any longer, does that means no one can speak in tongues today?

Those who say this, reason that though Phillip was in Samaria to preach Christ unto them as a result of which they received the gift of salvation, he had to send to Jerusalem to get Peter and John, one of the original Apostles to come lay hands on the new Christians at Samaria in order that they might receive the Holy Ghost. They assume that the reason why Peter and John were the ones who laid hands on the Samaritans was because Philip was not one of those Apostles present on the day of Pentecost.

They reason that only one of the Apostles present on the day of Pentecost could get other believers filled with the Holy Ghost.

There are some challenges with that argument.

> *And there was a certain disciple at Damascus, named Ananias; and to him said the Lord in a vision, Ananias. And he said, Behold, I am here, Lord. And Ananias went his way, and entered into the house; and putting his hands on him said, Brother Saul, the Lord, even Jesus, that appeared unto thee in the way as thou camest, hath sent me, that thou mightest receive thy sight, and be filled with the Holy Ghost.*

[ACTS 9:10,17]

The Lord Jesus persuaded Ananias to minister to Saul. Ananias told Saul, "the Lord, even Jesus, that appeared unto thee in the way as thou camest, hath sent me, that thou mightest receive thy sight, and be filled with the Holy Ghost" Acts 9.17.

Here's what we know from the record of the book of Acts:

Even if Ananias was present on the day of Pentecost, Ananias was simply introduced as a disciple not an Apostle.

It was this disciple that the Lord Jesus instructed to go lay hands on Saul, in order that Saul might be filled with the Holy Ghost.

We know Paul got filled because he said, "I thank my God I speak with tongues more than you all" (1 Cor. 14:18). The Lord Jesus used a disciple to get one of his own chosen vessels filled with the Holy Ghost! We therefore have scriptural evidence that believers, who are not Apostles, have the right to lay hands on other believers, in order that they might be filled with the Holy Ghost.

Apparently, Jesus knew nothing about this requirement that only an Apostle who was present on the day of Pentecost could do the job!

Consider also that Saul was not one of the original Apostles, nor was he a believer at Pentecost. He became a Christian and later an Apostle many years after Pentecost, yet we find him ministering by the laying on of hands to the saints at Ephesus. So, in the bible, both believers and Apostles laid hands in order that Christians might be filled with the Holy Ghost. The Lord honoured people's faith and expectancy. Peter and John were likely specialists who had a noted ability to minister to Christians by the laying on of hands (Acts 8:14). Phillip could have ministered the same way Ananias ministered but the Church is a body. We get the best results when we work as a team.

Question

What if I ask to be filled with the Spirit and I then start speaking in demonic tongues?

Spiritual rumor mongering as well as wrong teaching fuels the fear behind this particular question. It is a long-standing fear that was thankfully anticipated by the Lord Jesus and addressed in Luke's account.

In order to understand the passage in the book of Luke, you need to remember that Jesus had already given the disciples dominion over serpents, scorpions and all the power of the enemy (Luke 10:19). He was not discussing zoology. The serpents and scorpions symbolically refer to demons and evil spirits.

If a son shall ask bread of any of you that is a father, will he give him a stone? or if he ask a fish, will he for a fish give him a serpent? Or if he shall ask an egg, will he offer him a scorpion? If ye then, being evil, know how to give good gifts unto your children: how much more shall your heavenly Father give the Holy Spirit to them that ask him?

[LUKE 11:11-13]

He had fixed the meaning of serpent and scorpions in the chapter before this. When He says fathers would not offer serpent and scorpions in response to their children's request, He meant that God as our Father would definitely not give us evil spirits in response to our requests. We should not expect God as our Father to treat us worse than we would treat our own children, who ask us for food. Even imperfect and evil parents give the best to their children. If we as God's own sons ask our heavenly Father for the Holy Ghost, He will definitely not give an evil spirit. It is an absolute impossibility.

Question

I don't see eye to eye on many doctrinal issues with a particular church and in fact many of the members don't have solid characters but they speak in tongues. Surely that must mean that their tongues just like their character must be false?

In answering this, let's consider the following statements that Paul made concerning the Corinthian church:

That in every thing ye are enriched by him, in all utterance, and in all knowledge; So that ye come behind in no gift; waiting for the coming of our Lord Jesus Christ: For it hath been declared unto me of you, my brethren, by them which are of the house of Chloe, that there are contentions among you.

[1 CORINTHIANS 1:5,7,11]

For ye are yet carnal: for whereas there is among you envying, and strife, and divisions, are ye not carnal, and walk as men?

[1 CORINTHIANS 3:3]

It is the scandal of God's grace that the Corinthian Christians, with all their well-documented character flaws, still remained enriched by Jesus in all utterance and they also came behind in no gift! If it were up to us, we would find their character flaws such a turn off that we would not divide any manifestation of the Spirit to the Corinthian church, wouldn't we?

It is a sobering thought that there will be genuine manifestations and operations of the Spirit of God among groups that we don't see eye to eye with (and maybe they also do not see eye to eye with us). God is more merciful than we allow for and He does not tow denominational lines when choosing if He will show up among a group or not. If they are believers in Christ Jesus, then they are sons of the Father and if they in spite of their flaws desire the things of the Spirit, then the Holy Ghost has enough reason to show up and He most definitely will.

The Corinthian church were blinded by cliques and factions, getting drunk on communion wine and giving themselves over to unprintable abominations, some of which Paul said could not be even named among unbelievers. While Paul was aware of these, he did not once write to them to discontinue speaking in tongues, lest a demon that was unwittingly yielded to them starts manifesting "false" tongues through the wayward believers amongst them. Paul's counsel to the Corinthian crowd was,

> *"Wherefore, brethren, covet to prophesy, and forbid not to speak with tongues"*
>
> [1 CORINTHIANS 14:39]

Paul corrected the excesses of carnal Christians but he never sowed any seed of doubt in their hearts about the genuineness of their tongues. If people are carnal or are even in one form of error or another, we still don't have scriptural grounds to tell them to stop speaking in tongues because we suppose that their tongues must be false. Rather, we should point them to the Word that is able to cleanse them. The

Word of God strengthens them against the flesh and restores their soul.

We are to place our trust on the Word and not in our misconceptions about the genuineness of their tongues. What some Christians peddle in the name of discernment is nothing more than the age-old gift of suspicion! Let's remember the way the Spirit guided Paul to deal with the carnal Corinthians and follow his godly example.

The Holy Spirit does not require moral perfection in the life of a believer before He can move. If God were to demand doctrinal perfection or moral excellence as a pre-requisite for speaking in tongues, then who would qualify?

Apostle Peter was filled with the Holy Ghost and had been speaking in tongues for many years before God showed him in a vision that Gentiles were not to be treated as common (Acts 10:15). While in a trance, God had to show him a vision three times, coupled with additional persuasion from the Holy Spirit before Peter would go to Cornelius' house (Acts 10:20). Praise God all those years of praying in tongues and fellowshipping with God did pay off though – He was yielded enough to God to go to Cornelius in spite of his prejudices against Gentiles.

Therefore on the day of Pentecost, Apostle Peter held strong prejudices against the Gentiles but this did not stop the Lord Jesus from filling him with the Holy Ghost! Peter continued to speak in tongues while still holding onto his prejudices against Gentiles, believing that gentiles had no right to salvation. He was not alone in this bigotry, for after he ministered to Cornelius and his household Peter faced a panel for preaching to Gentiles (Acts 11:2)! As far as we can tell, all the leaders of the Jerusalem church, who were the leaders of that panel, spoke in tongues. It must have hurt God's heart that the Christians were bound by deep-seated prejudice but this did not deter Him from filling them.

But when Peter was come to Antioch, I withstood him to the face, because he was to be blamed.

[GALATIANS 2:11]

Many years after the Cornelius episode, Peter still manifested some of his prejudice. He joined a clique of bigots that would not eat with Gentile brethren. In spite of all these flaws, the Holy Ghost still filled him and continued to use him mightily!

Wherever people desire the spiritual things of God, the Spirit of God finds liberty for expression. If we don't desire the spiritual things of God, no matter how solid our character, the manifestations of the Spirit will be fewer and far between if any at all.

Question

What is speaking in tongues?

For if I pray in an unknown tongue, my spirit prayeth, but my understanding is unfruitful.

[1 CORINTHIANS 14:14]

Speaking in tongues is a conversation between our recreated spirits and our Father God. The Holy Spirit places the utterance within the spirit mind. Speaking in tongues is yielding your physical tongue to your spiritual tongue, so you can speak spiritual utterances. In anatomical terms, your will moves your biological tongue to push out as audible sounds the utterance that is in the spiritual mind. We refer to these sounds as speaking in tongues. You'll come to pick up the utterances that become tongues with your spiritual ear. The utterances are not accessible through the biological ear but through the spiritual ear. Your biological ear can pick up the sounds that you speak in tongues only after your mouth has uttered it. You don't hear the Holy Spirit supplying the utterance to you in your biological ear.

Question

The unbeliever is a spirit being and speaking in tongues is our spirit speaking. Why then don't unbelievers speak in tongues?

> *And they were all filled with the Holy Ghost, and began to speak with other tongues, as the Spirit gave them utterance.*
>
> [ACTS 2:4]

In order to understand this enigma, you must remember that speaking in tongues is speaking as the indwelling Holy Spirit gives man utterance. Speaking in tongues is a communication channel that God has specifically given to His spirit-filled sons. When speaking in tongues, the tongues itself is spoken by the spirit of man but the indwelling Holy Spirit generates the language or gives the utterance. The spirit of the unbeliever can speak but it cannot be diversities of tongues because the human spirit is not born again, therefore the Holy Spirit does not indwell it. The man who is not born again cannot bear the utterance that becomes tongues for he does not have a nature with which to receive it.

Question

I have received eternal life and now I want to speak in tongues. Why has God not given it to me?

A principle to remember is that whenever people were to be filled with the Holy Ghost in the bible, the emphasis was not on the God side. It is never an issue of God giving. This is obvious from the question that Paul asked when he came in contact with the fellows at Ephesus. He assumed that they were believers in Christ.

> *He said unto them, Have ye received the Holy Ghost since ye believed? And they said unto him, We have not so much as heard whether there be any Holy Ghost.*
>
> [ACTS 19:2]

Paul did not ask them, "Has God given you the Holy Ghost?" It is a question of receiving as God has already made the provision. The Holy Ghost is already available. What he asked was, "Have you received the Holy Ghost?" Our believing does not make God give, it helps us receive from God.

See the following account of when Peter and John were sent to the Samaritan Christians to help them with the infilling of the Holy Spirit.

> *Now when the apostles which were at Jerusalem heard that Samaria had received the word of God, they sent unto them Peter and John: Who, when they were come down, prayed for them, that they might receive the Holy Ghost:*
>
> [ACTS 8:14-15]

That term "received the word" refers to the New Birth. Notice that Peter and John did not ask God to do anything. They prayed for the new believers but the prayer was in order to get the Samaritans receive the Holy Ghost.

Peter and John had a ministry along the lines of ministering the Holy Ghost by the laying on of hands. When they laid hands, it is interesting to see how the bible describes what was going on.

> *Then laid they their hands on them, and they received the Holy Ghost.*
>
> [ACTS 8:17]

Peter and John laid hands.

The Samaritan Christians now received the Holy Ghost through the ministry of Peter and John just like they had received the Word earlier through the ministry of Phillip.

The emphasis for both the New Birth and getting filled with the Spirit is on the receiving side – man's side.

According to Paul, when I speak in tongues "my understanding is unfruitful" 1 Cor. 14:14. This means that the mind is not the engine behind speaking in tongues. Failing to understand this, most people who are looking for the infilling of the Holy Spirit look to their natural mind to produce sounds in a known language. This hinders them from speaking in tongues.

While you can hear other people speak in tongues through your biological ear, you don't hear the Holy Spirit supplying the utterance to you in your biological ear. If you are listening for the utterance with your physical ear, you will wait forever. The utterances that become tongues are not accessible through your biological ear but through the spiritual ear or eye. The primary characteristic of speaking in tongues is that the tongues totally bypass your physical mind; so don't look to your mind.

When it comes to speaking in tongues, the sequence is as follows. The Holy Spirit places the utterance within your spirit mind. You then set your will to speak by faith knowing that the utterance is there already in your spiritual tongue and you deliberately use your physical tongue to complete the cycle by releasing the sound audibly. That is what you use your faith for when you want to speak in tongues as a result of being filled with the Holy Spirit.

Question

I have friends who have repeatedly asked God to fill them with the Holy Spirit. Why are they not yet filled?

There is a remedy for such friends. Help your friends understand that the Father can be trusted to do what He has said in His Word. He gives the Holy Spirit to all who ask Him (Luke 11:13). Since they asked, God has given them the Holy Spirit! In reality, God does not give the Holy Spirit because we ask. He has already given the Holy

Spirit. We ask in order to receive. On the practical side, people think that since they have not spoken in tongues it is because God has not answered. The problem has to do with what they believe as well as their yieldedness.

> Nay, some one will say, "You have faith, I have actions: prove to me your faith apart from corresponding actions and I will prove mine to you by my actions. For just as a human body without a spirit is lifeless, so also faith is lifeless if it is unaccompanied by obedience.
>
> [JAMES 2:18,26 - WEYMOUTH]

It was an act of faith that made them ask the Lord Jesus to fill them with the Holy Spirit in the first place. They do not need to keep asking the Lord Jesus to fill them for they already asked in faith. Now they need to believe that they have received the infilling (Mk. 11:24) and then prove their faith by acting correspondingly. They are to act correspondingly to their faith by speaking; otherwise, their faith will be lifeless and void. It will not produce the desired result because they have not spoken, not because they are not filled. Those who are filled with the Spirit speak. The litmus test is this, "when will they move from asking to speaking?"

> He said unto them, Have ye received the Holy Ghost since ye believed? And they said unto him, We have not so much as heard whether there be any Holy Ghost.
>
> [ACTS 19:2]

What was it that caused Paul to ask these folks, "Have you received the Holy Ghost since ye believed?" He assumed that they had believed and received but that something was not adding up. It is obvious they were not speaking in tongues. This would be the obvious way of telling.

The answer of the Ephesians is illuminating. They said, "We have not so much as heard whether there be any Holy Ghost". They were ignorant about the things of the Spirit. They therefore did not know how to receive. Paul then proceeded to instruct them. People generally receive better when they have clear instructions.

Explain to those who want to get filled with the Spirit that since the things they will say will not come from their minds, you are guaranteeing them that it will sound weird to their mind. They need to be hundred percent certain about this. Let them know that the thing they are about to say will sound foolish but that God understands and their spirits get the gist of it. They should proceed by releasing a sound that demonstrates their faith in God's Word.

And they were all filled with the Holy Ghost, and began to speak with other tongues, as the Spirit gave them utterance.

[ACTS 2:4]

They should follow the well-established bible pattern of beginning to speak in other tongues. Their physical mind should not be in control; for the physical mind only knows the languages that it has been taught. They are to believe God's Word that the Father has given them the Holy Spirit. They are to then receive by faith in God's Word. They then set their will that they will not allow their mind get in the way as they open their mouths to push out sounds other than their every day speech. This means they are to continue to believe that the words that will come out of their mouths in a language other than their vernacular is the utterance of the Holy Spirit.

Question
What is the purpose of all the mysteries that I speak in tongues?

When you speak in tongues, it totally bypasses your physical mind (1 Cor. 14:14). The primal reason why our physical mind is bypassed is because our minds are not totally renewed with the Word of God. The limitations in knowledge exist in our physical mind and it is this limitation of know-how that enforces the inadequacies we grapple with in daily life. The help the Holy Spirit gives comes as an utterance.

The Holy Spirit inspired utterance is within your spiritual mind and as you speak it out with your physical tongue, you are exchanging secrets with God. The things spoken are not secrets to God but to you. It's just like your spirit is in the classroom and your spiritual understanding is getting a download. When you keep communicating with God this way over extended periods, it becomes easier for the download to flow from your spiritual mind to your natural mind. The continual download of mysteries means that the understanding within your natural mind is now the spiritual understanding that was within your spiritual mind. You have renewed your natural mind with solid information from your spiritual mind.

Question

What are the tests for identifying whether a believer's tongues are genuine?

While the bible gives a lot of instructions concerning the subject of tongues, God did not directly or indirectly give us any criteria for evaluating the genuineness of tongues. Paul wrote entire chapters about tongues but did not once treat the subject of how we determine the genuineness of tongues. Clearly, if God had thought it important, He would have given us instructions about it. There is no benefit in trying to establish the genuineness of anyone's tongues otherwise the matter would have been treated. We go beyond the bound of scripture when we try to determine whether the tongues spoken by a righteous one who believes in Christ Jesus, are genuine. Any such attempt is fanciful and speculatory at best.

If a son shall ask bread of any of you that is a father, will he give him a stone? or if he ask a fish, will he for a fish give him a serpent? Or if he shall ask an egg, will he offer him a scorpion? If ye then, being evil, know how to give good gifts unto your children: how much more shall your heavenly Father give the Holy Spirit to them that ask him?

[LUKE 11:11-13]

The Lord Jesus gives us iron clad assurance as to the impossibility of receiving a demon empowered tongue when receiving the infilling of the Holy Spirit. It is simply impossible. God would not give an evil spirit to the believer who reaches out to Him in this regard. Even if the Christian is immature, we know that our Father God takes His responsibility as a Father seriously enough to guarantee that such would never happen. Someone says "but there are demons everywhere". A Christian should trust more in the Father reality, than in demonic presence.

Question

What if my tongues are not valid?

I was startled the first time it dawned on me that the apostle Paul in all his writings does not once warn us against false tongues. Surely he should have known if false tongues exist for the believer in Christ Jesus. Satan persecutes with this idea of false tongues and there are countless tongue talkers who have been plagued with this thought through the ages. This is really one that should be fairly easy to answer. The apostle Paul that the Lord used to give instructions about speaking with tongues did not ever infer that there could be invalid tongues.

In all his instructions, he implies that we face the real danger of the invalid exercise of tongues but does not once say that the tongues itself is invalid or false.

Question

On the day of Pentecost there were cloven tongues of fire as well as a sound of a rushing wind but when I see people being ministered to in Churches that believe speaking in tongues is valid today, these ingredients are missing. Are they not promoting a satanic delusion?

This is one of those molehills that people try to make a mountain out of but in the light of scriptures, it remains insignificant. People who say this have Acts 2 in mind. If we are going to insist on Acts 2 as the template, then we should apply the full Acts 2 template. If we are going to insist on the sound of the rushing mighty wind and cloven tongues of fire, everyone who needs to get filled with the spirit must also first go to Jerusalem and wait for the day of Pentecost. The cloven tongues of fire, Jerusalem and the Feast of Pentecost all go together.

If we should apply this logic to preaching the Gospel of Salvation, since the first recorded gospel message was in Jerusalem, what do I do if I meet someone on the streets of London in need of salvation? Do I insist on first flying out that sinner to Jerusalem for the feast of Pentecost? Do I then wait for the third hour of the day to pass before I preach to the sinner? That is futility gone to seed!

The fact, from the book of Acts, is that Peter and John did not place emphasis on the rushing wind and cloven tongues of fire at Samaria, nor did Paul insist on it in Ephesus. The cloven tongues is not a requirement nor is it a stamp of genuineness.

There was a variety in the experience of those who spoke in tongues in the book of Acts. In Acts 2 and Acts 10, no hands were laid on anyone, though all that were filled spoke in tongues. On the other hand, in both Acts 8 and Acts 19 hands were laid on those who became filled with the Spirit and started speaking in tongues. In Acts 10, they spoke in tongues before they got baptised in water, whereas in Acts 19 they spoke in tongues after they were baptised in water. Who baptised the 120 before they started speaking in tongues at Pentecost?

In Acts 10, there is no mention of cloven tongues as of fire or a rushing mighty wind. What convinced the Jewish Christians was that they heard the Gentiles in Cornelius' house speak in tongues (Acts 10:46). In Acts 19, there's also no mention of cloven tongues as of fire or a rushing mighty wind. Paul laid hands on the believers, who then spoke in tongues and prophesied.

The commonality was that all who were filled with the Spirit were Christians by the time they started speaking in tongues. Otherwise, there is no pattern that is consistent in all the records we find in the book of Acts. The only thing worth emphasising is speaking as a result of being filled.

Question

What about people who appear to be repeating the same sounds over and over?

This is an often-voiced sentiment that gives speaking in tongues a sense of fabrication since a repetition of same sound sequence is observable in many who speak in tongues. Many people who speak in tongues but find themselves repeating the same set of syllables are sometimes perplexed as to the genuineness of their expression. They allow the enemy capitalize on their ignorance and rob them of confidence when speaking in tongues. If left unchecked, many abandon speaking in tongues altogether because the enemy injects thoughts into their minds that they are involved in something phoney but is it so?

While correcting the Corinthians, Paul cited Isaiah's prophecy, "For with stammering lips and another tongue will he speak to this people" (Isaiah 28:11) as the foundation for speaking in tongues. Isaiah not only talks about other tongues but about stammering lips as well. They go hand in hand. He therefore endorses stammering lips as a valid demonstration of speaking in tongues. This means that when we speak in tongues, we might not start out fluently. It is as scriptural to stammer in tongues, as it is to speak in tongues.

Isaiah's prophecy allows for everything in between stammering and fluent speech. It basically means that there is a progression in these spiritual utterances. Just as with everyday vernacular, one becomes a better speaker with practice; the one who speaks in tongues will improve with use. By extension, a person who seldom speaks in tongues might find that he is limited in his vocabulary in tongues because of insufficient exercise. Keep practicing and with your mastery you will gain confidence. You will become better at yielding to the Holy Spirit for clearer articulation as well as a wider vocabulary range as you speak in tongues.

If you keep repeating the same syllables in tongues, that does not make your tongues fake. Little children trying to learn a new language often repeat the new sounds of that language. They do not start with the full dictionary but with a few words. Your range expands with practice.

Our vocabulary is as wide as our yielding allows. If you yield the same way you have always yielded and as far as you have always yielded, guess what? You will utter the same syllables. If you yield more, you open up yourself to a fuller expression.

What is interesting is that as you yield to the Holy Ghost in other areas of life, you would discover that it helps you yield to Him, when it comes to utterance in tongues also.

Question

I have listened to some people's tongues and it is not one of the languages of the earth. Surely their tongues is not genuine?

> *And they were all filled with the Holy Ghost, and began to speak with other tongues, as the Spirit gave them utterance.*
>
> [ACTS 2:4]

On the day of Pentecost, all the disciples spoke with tongues. We are not told that some spoke in tongues while others examined, validated, classified or identified what nations of the earth the languages spoken came from. They would not know what to expect when they started speaking in tongues, since no one in history had spoken in tongues. There was no precedence to go by. They busied themselves speaking in tongues and not in trying to identify what portion of the earth the language originated from. Let's mimic their example in this respect.

For he that speaketh in an unknown tongue speaketh not unto men, but unto God: for no man understandeth him; howbeit in the spirit he speaketh mysteries.

[1 CORINTHIANS 14:2]

The primary use of tongues is for conversations with God and to supernaturally enrich our spiritual worship of God. Speaking in tongues in its everyday usage in the life of the believing one is for conversations between the spirit of a reborn man and the Spirit of God. This exchange is a deep spiritual communion between man's own spirit and God. The known languages of the earth are of the mind of men. It is one human mind speaking to another but tongues is between man and God. This conversation is a two-way street. It is man speaking to God and God speaking back to man as part of a rich communion. When speaking in tongues is in the man-speaking-to-God mode, there is no need for any interpretation. However, when it is God speaking to man, someone needs to interpret the response of God, in order that the hearer might understand and receive edification.

When people argue that the language spoken does not match any which is spoken on the earth, how can they be sure? We must not shy away from the reality of linguicide, which is the literal extinction of a language or dialect. This happens, when there are no living native speakers of a language. Linguists tell us that there are many human languages that have gone extinct since ancient times and many even recently. Some estimate that there are about seven thousand or more distinct tongues spoken in the world today, half of which could disappear within the next 100 years.

Take for example the case of Papa New Guinea, a nation of under 7 million people who speak about 848 languages of which 12 are extinct, 36 are dying and 800 are still widely spoken to the present day. One of those languages, like Abaga, is spoken by as few as five people. If those five die in an accident, that language is dead. Fifty years after their death, if that happens to be what someone speaks in tongues there will be some fellow who will jump up and declare that what is spoken does not match any language known to man! It is beyond the ability of any man alive today to tell conclusively that the language spoken is not human.

Though I speak with the tongues of men and of angels, and have not charity, I am become as sounding brass, or a tinkling cymbal.

[1 CORINTHIANS 13:1]

Even if it were the case that the language was not human, the apostle Paul made allowance for the tongues of angels, which refer to heavenly languages. The tongues that the typical spirit-filled Christian would speak would be the tongues of angels. This is the tongues of edification and praise. When the tongue spoken is known to someone present, that is a sign to the one that understands its meaning. It is a valid use of tongues but that is the exception and not the norm. No one can claim to be an expert in locating and classifying the dialects and phonetics of angelic speech.

There is nothing in the design of tongues that demands tongues to be a known language, or a language ever spoken by any human in any age. It is the human spirit expressing itself to God and drawing out edification for man's whole constitution. You get edified by actually speaking in tongues and not for correctly identifying what region of the universe the language is from.

There is no gift of the spirit called "identifying the region that the tongue is from". As far as we can tell from scriptures, there is no advantage to be gained from being able to identify which part of the earth that the spoken language is from.

He that speaketh in a tongue that someone around him can identify shall be built up spiritually and until someone identifies it his edification

is suspended
[1 CORINTHIANS 14:4 - THE FANCIFUL VERSION]

There is no translation like the one above.

Question

Surely we should speak in tongues only when the Holy Spirit's grip on us is so strong that we have no hiding place for us. If tongues is not ecstatic, surely it is not of God and not genuine, is it?

Those who believe that speaking in tongues is ecstatic utterance think that it should only be exercised when people whip up intense psychological frenzy and an intense emotional overload, resulting in a loss of self-control at which point they burst forth in other tongues. They think that this is the recipe that guarantees to the person speaking in tongues as well as other believers, the divine component of speaking in tongues.

Let's first define ecstatic.

According to the Oxford dictionary, it is a state of being beyond reason and self-control.

Does God endorse this?

> *For with stammering lips and another tongue will he speak to this people. To whom he said, This is the rest wherewith ye may cause the weary to rest; and this is the refreshing: yet they would not hear.*
> [ISAIAH 28.11-12]

God inspired Isaiah to prophesy a future age when men would speak in tongues. According to Isaiah's prophecy, speaking in tongues will not be a frenzied, mindless, loss-of-self-control kind of experience but a refreshing and a rest to the speaker. The kind of speaking in tongues anticipated in prophecy by Isaiah, is the sort that calms the mind without working it into a frenzied state. It has nothing to do with emotional overload. Expecting to be in a frenzied state before you can speak in tongues is a learned behaviour and is a product of what we are taught or practices we have observed in the circles we walk in.

Consider the first occurrence of actual speaking in tongues in the bible,

> *And they were all filled with the Holy Ghost, and began to speak with other tongues, as the Spirit gave them utterance.*
> [ACTS 2:4]

That expression, "as the Holy Spirit gave them utterance", means that the Holy Ghost supplied the supernatural ability for the believer's spirit to say the tongues. This is not ecstatic at all but speaking by inspiration. This is the same principle by which men of old wrote scriptures under inspiration.

> *All scripture is given by inspiration of God, and is profitable for doctrine, for reproof, for correction, for instruction in righteousness:*
> [2 TIMOTHY 3.16]

The same Sprit that inspired the writing of scripture is the one that inspires the fellow leading worship in church and it is this same inspiration that is behind tongues. The major difference between the inspiration of tongues and that of writing scripture is the degree of inspiration. The degree of inspiration is highest in the writing of scripture. Many consider speaking in tongues to be ecstatic utterance because they confuse inspiration for ecstasy. God does not encourage ecstatic speaking, if by that we mean speech arising from overwhelming emotion marked by absence of self-control. God has always employed inspiration. He wants us to exercise self-control (2 Tim. 1:7, 1 Pet. 4:7, Titus 1:8).

If speaking in tongues is to be ecstatic like some believe, then there is no reason for the instructions that God gave through Paul in 1 Corinthians 14. For by the time we are speaking it is guaranteed that we would have lost self-control any way and would be functioning beyond reason. In such a state, we blame our excesses on God, for He is the one supposedly moving us and we are not in control!

The very existence of those instructions is proof that we can do something about administering speaking in tongues. We do not lose control or go beyond reason. We are in control of our faculties. It is just that the language is not flowing from our head. Our will is involved all the way (1 Cor. 14:15).

> *If any man speak in an unknown tongue, let it be by two, or at the most by three, and that by course; and let one interpret. But if there be no interpreter, let him keep silence in the church; and let him speak to himself, and to God.*
>
> [1 CORINTHIANS 14:27-28]

The instruction to keep silent in the church, while speaking to yourself and to God means that the fellow speaking in tongues is in control of how loud he sounds, whether he will raise his voice for the whole church to hear or keep it low just for himself. He is also sober enough to know, whether the interpreter is around or not. This means that the one speaking in tongues, even when he feels that he has a message for the church, must retain self-control. Otherwise, he would blurt out everything that comes to him in a frenzy to whoever is around him without retaining the ability to determine when to speak, how loud to speak, who to speak to and when not to speak.

There is such a thing as ecstatic tongues practiced by some but it stems from wrong thinking, wrong believing and practice. The emotional frenzy and loss of self-control criteria is really of the flesh, so it is carnal and lends itself to the type of confusing atmosphere that demons like. The thing to remember is that wherever the human will is breached, the wrong kind of spirits could be released and commissioned – God is the Author of peace, decency and order (1

Cor. 14:40). You should not find ecstatic tongues in church or in your private life nor should any believer strive for it. It is not a mark of spirituality or maturity but of infancy.

Question

What of those who get really loud and wild when speaking in tongues? Is that genuine?

> *If any man speak in an unknown tongue, let it be by two, or at the most by three, and that by course; and let one interpret. But if there be no interpreter, let him keep silence in the church; and let him speak to himself, and to God.*
>
> ### [1 CORINTHIANS 14:27-28]

When Paul penned those instructions "let him keep silence", he was not instructing God. Those instructions were for us. God does not control the amplification of our voice when we speak in tongues, though we like to think He does. He does not decide to be quiet at some times and be loud at other times. God does not have mood swings, we do. We are the ones who respond to God in a loud voice sometimes and in a more quiet voice at other times. There is nothing wrong with the raised voice or the quiet whisper but each has its proper setting.

Without a doubt, some wildness shines through when some people speak in tongues. It is not the tongues that makes them wild; they always had the wildness in them. I have seen gentle people get wild when speaking in tongues and I have also seen wild people speak in tongues in calm gentle tones. A principle to remember is that the spirit of the prophet is subject to the prophet (1 Cor. 14:32). There is a lot that goes on during supernatural manifestations that expresses the personality of the one being used of God. God is responsible for supplying inspiration to the fellow speaking in tongues but the fellow is responsible for pretty much everything afterwards. The reason why my tongues might sound louder than yours is down to variations in our personality and not variations in God. The variation that you might have noticed in the execution of supernatural manifestation is because God does not supress our personality but uses as much of it as we make available to him.

God is not out to destroy you but to express Himself through you in your own unique way. There is nothing wrong with raising your voice while speaking in tongues once you understand that you are the one determining the amplification in your voice. It is your voice responding to God's inspiration. The wildness on display was not from God but the expression of the human element. It is acceptable for as long as we do not think that our animated responses are a pre-requisite for its "supernaturalness". As we grow up spiritually, we renew our minds; gain more control of our soul and generally the wildness disappears and true spiritual strength is demonstrated.

Question

I really want to pray in tongues, and I have been waiting for God to do something about it and He has chosen not to make me speak! Am I unworthy?

People who hold on to the sentiment that they are waiting for God to do something about their speaking in tongues are really waiting for something quite spectacular. This is equivalent to someone saying that he is not yet saved because he is waiting for God to do something about his salvation. Just as no one is really waiting for God to get him or her born again, no one can scripturally be waiting for God to make him or her speak in tongues. The major hindrance to their speaking in tongues is that they think that it is up to God whether they will speak in tongues or not. This is largely because they have not been instructed that they are the ones that will begin to speak in tongues and not God (Acts 2:4). If there is any kind of timing involved, it is their timing and not God's. The blood of Jesus has made you worthy, and in God's eyes that blood is enough (1 Cor. 6:11); but is the blood enough for you in your own eyes?

But ye, beloved, building up yourselves on your most holy faith, praying in the Holy Ghost,

[JUDE 20]

In chemistry, we learnt about catalysts. Sometimes you have substances that do not react with one another when exposed to each other. When you introduce the catalyst, it does not create the different substances but it creates an atmosphere for increased reactions to take place. Speaking in tongues is like a spiritual catalyst. It does not create faith but it causes a reaction between the faith of God and you to release tremendous power of God.

Building up yourself on your most holy faith means you are able to maximize the faith that is stirred up in you by the Word of God. It is the Word that imparts faith but as we pray in tongues, we build ourselves up on that faith so that we can maximize our faith. You are building your consciousness of the faith of Christ that is at your disposal. You could have all the faith in the universe but if you do not gain a consciousness of it, you would not be able to maximize that faith. Speaking in tongues helps you use what is yours.

These be they who separate themselves, sensual, having not the Spirit.

[JUDE 19]

The sensual are those whose reality flows from whatever their eyes, ears, nose and tongue tells them. These people are separating themselves from the original revelation given through the Apostles in the Word. Speaking in tongues is a catalyst that builds us up, above sensuality and deception because of the Word of God deposited within us. Speaking in tongues must never be a substitute for staying full of God's Word.

8

Instructions for getting filled

Most Christians have a challenge when it comes to initially getting filled with the Holy Ghost. When Paul got to Ephesus (Acts 19), he did not just walk over, lay hands on the Ephesians and command them to start speaking in tongues. He engaged them in conversation until he discovered where their challenge lay. We are to do all that we can in order to help people receive. In the case of these Ephesians, they had zero information about the subject matter for they said, "We have not heard whether there be a Holy Ghost"!

Here are some instructions to help those who are in a hurry:

And they were all filled with the Holy Ghost, and began to speak with other tongues, as the Spirit gave them utterance.

[ACTS 2:4]

Here are some facts to take note of:

1. The Holy Ghost did not get filled with the Holy Ghost.
2. The Holy Ghost did not receive the Holy Ghost.
3. The Holy Ghost did not speak in tongues.
4. The believers got filled with the Holy Ghost.
5. The believers received the Holy Ghost.
6. The believers spoke in tongues.
7. The Holy Ghost filled them.
8. The Holy Ghost gave them utterance.

Therefore speaking in tongues is not just about the believer, neither is it just up to the Holy Ghost. It is cooperation between the believer and the Holy Ghost.

The Holy Ghost as a gift to be received

For the promise is unto you, and to your children, and to all that are afar off, even as many as the LORD our God shall call.

[ACTS 2:39]

The promise that Peter quoted was a promise unto three sets of people; the first category was the Jews that Peter was addressing that day. The second category was their children and the third category included those that are afar off, even as many as the Lord would call – that third group includes those reading this book.

Peter was speaking by inspiration of the Holy Ghost. He did not know that "all that are afar off" included the Gentiles. His spirit was aware of a revelation that his mind had not yet understood. Just because you say something out of your mouth does not mean you grasp it.

Well, what promise has he just guaranteed to all those who the Lord shall call?

Then Peter said unto them, Repent, and be baptized every one of you in the name of Jesus Christ for the remission of sins, and ye shall receive the gift of the Holy Ghost.

[ACTS 2:38]

It was the promise of the Holy Ghost as a gift.

What do we do with gifts? We receive them.

Peter said that his hearers, who believed the word that he was preaching, were to receive the gift of the Holy Ghost.

This is why you find that in the book of Acts the predominant term used was that of "receiving the Holy Ghost" for the gift is already given.

The single most important fact that could help you in getting filled with the Spirit is that the Holy Ghost is a gift. You do not work for gifts. You receive with thanksgiving. You are not scoring any brownie points that will make God give you the Holy Ghost. As with any area of our walk as believers, we must know the God part as well as the man side to being filled with the Holy Ghost. We know this through the Word.

He gives the utterance, we do the praying

I thank my God, I speak with tongues more than ye all:

[1 CORINTHIANS 14:18]

The Apostle Paul gives priceless information here. He did not say, "I thank my God that God speaks in tongues through me more than …" He thanked God that he (Paul) spoke in tongues and not that God spoke in tongues. While the Holy Ghost speaks; He does not speak in tongues. I find that once I can get this singular point across to the people I minister to, they usually end up yielding to God and speaking with tongues knowing that they are the ones speaking!

And they of the circumcision which believed were astonished, as many as came with Peter, because that on the Gentiles also was poured out the gift of the Holy Ghost.

[ACTS 10:45]

And they were all filled with the Holy Spirit, and began to speak with strange 'tongues' as the Spirit prompted their utterances

[ACTS 2:4 - TCNT]

It is one thing to be prompted but altogether a different matter for us to act on it. It is not that the Holy Ghost prompts some but not others. The observable difference is what believers do with the prompting. Failing to act on that prompting is the singular reason why people get ministered to and they end up not speaking in tongues. Speaking is something man has always done. There is nothing supernatural about a human being speaking but there is a whole new dimension of blessing when man speaks as a result of the inspiration and prompting of the Holy Ghost. This urge (or prompting) usually registers on the physical tongue but does not become a flowing stream until you begin to speak sounds other than your everyday vernacular.

The Holy Ghost supplied the utterance. He did not force their mouth open, move their tongue up and down, take over their voice box or push sounds out of their mouth.

The Holy Ghost is our Helper. He helps us do the speaking. He does not do the speaking for us.

Who will speak? You will.

Whose mouth will open? Yours will.

Who will open your mouth? You will.

Who will push out the sounds? You will.

What will the Holy Ghost do? He will see to it that you get all the prompting and urge you need.

What of those who say, "I prefer the Holy Ghost to do the speaking. I am more comfortable with that"? Well, the Holy Ghost definitely prefers you to do the talking. He is much more comfortable with that – and He is right! He will give you utterance as well as inspire the content of what you speak in tongues but the Holy Spirit does not do the actual speaking in tongues. Too many Christians think the speaking is also supernatural, so they are waiting for the Holy Ghost to take over and do the speaking. Even if the Holy Spirit could speak in tongues, His speaking it out would not make it any more supernatural than your speaking it out. I cannot tell you how many people I have come across who were bound by that thought, they have been taught to allow the Holy Ghost speak. They therefore believe along those lines and often wait forever.

Whatever you do, speak!

Remember that you are a spirit being with a spiritual mind. This spiritual mind is housed within your natural mind. It is in your spiritual mind that the Holy Spirit literally creates the syllables of other tongues. Don't spend your time thinking about the syllables or the urge. It's not thinking in tongues that you want, you want speaking in tongues – so speak!

Many people actually get filled with the Spirit but tend to quickly revert to responding to that urge by doing the things that those that are recognised as spiritual people in their denomination do. This varies from denomination to denomination and from church to church. Say for example, they come from a church where the really spiritual people grab the nearest flag and run around the church, you might find people from such background grab the nearest flag when they are filled with the Spirit. No, the Holy Spirit did not make them grab that flag; they are just responding, as they best know how. There's absolutely nothing wrong with grabbing flags and running round the church auditorium, if it is acceptable in a particular church. If you came forward to receive the Holy Ghost, then you should channel that anointing into speaking in a language that you have not learnt before. Once you have responded by speaking in other tongues, you are at liberty to pick up the flag and run around, but not before.

Now get ready to be filled with the spirit.

Believing and yielding

The two-fold challenge that exist in the area of being filled with the Holy Ghost tends to be either that of wrong believing or for those that believe rightly, a challenge arising from their degree of yielding to the utterance that the Holy Ghost will supply.

Unbelief is mostly faith exercised in the wrong things we believe about a subject. This type of unbelief is sustained by lack of knowledge, inaccurate knowledge or limiting traditions about getting filled with the Spirit. In order to overcome this unbelief and start believing correctly, read every single instance in the book of Acts where people spoke in tongues (See Chapter 6 of this book). Faith comes by hearing God's Word concerning being filled with the Holy Spirit (Rom. 10:17).

Another type of unbelief is fed by fear. This type of unbelief is a refusal to act on the Word that you know because things are not easy (Heb. 3:15). This is disobedience. It prevents us from reaping the benefits that are ours in Christ (Heb. 3:19).

We are already richly blessed with all spiritual blessings in the heavenly places in Christ (Eph. 1:3). The Holy Ghost has been given as a gift; therefore He is available and has been available since the day of Pentecost for the benefit of all and any member of the body of Christ. You qualify to receive the Holy Ghost if you are a member of the body of Christ. The New Birth qualifies you (See Acts 11:17, Acts 2:38). Now, let's see three methods for receiving:

Releasing your faith by saying

Bible faith receives from God and you release it through spoken words (Mk. 11:23). Believe with your heart that the Holy Ghost is available for you in a greater measure. Then release your faith by saying with your mouth, "I now receive the Holy Ghost into my life at this very instant as I speak these words from my heart." (2 Cor. 4:13, Mt. 12:34). From then on, keep saying to yourself that you now have the gift. This will help your consciousness. Whatever you are conscious of becomes bigger in your world.

Releasing your faith by praying

Just as you can exercise bible faith by saying, you can also exercise it by praying (Mk. 11:24). You can say something similar to the following:

I thank you Father God that
The Lord Jesus has supplied the Holy Ghost to me
The Lord Jesus is available to me today
And because I believe on the Lord Jesus,
The Holy Ghost is available to me today
He is the gift from the Lord Jesus to me
I now receive this gift by faith in your Word
I therefore believe that I am filled with God
Now, I believe that I am filled with the Holy Ghost
I also thank you for the Holy Ghost is already giving me utterance
By faith in Your Word, I will now speak in other tongues
And you know what Father I'll take whatever else You deem fit for me.

Releasing your faith by having hands laid on you

The Holy Ghost can also be received by the laying on of hands. This acts as a point of contact to help you release your faith to receive the Holy Ghost. You believe and say, "The instant that hands are laid on me, I will receive the Holy Ghost".

You are the one receiving

Remember you are the one receiving the Holy Ghost. If it were up to God to make you receive the Holy Ghost, He would have done so already. He does not make you do anything. He wants you to relax and yield to Him. Don't say, "I want it to be God". God wants it to be you. It is the one that does the receiving that also does the speaking. You are the one that will be speaking in tongues.

Don't speak unbelief by saying, "Perhaps because of this sin or that I will not receive" for that is exactly how the devil reasons and he wants you to reason like him in unbelief. If you reason and believe that way, you are exercising faith in reverse that you will not receive. Keep saying, "According to God's Word, I have spoken and I believe in my heart that I have now received the Holy Ghost".

At this point, you have received the gift of the Holy Ghost by faith. This is not make-believe but an actual reception. The Holy Ghost now clearly supplies utterance. This utterance will register like a desire, an inward compulsion or urge for you to say syllables, which would appear to sound like "rubbish", simply because they are sounds that are not your everyday speech. Zero in on sensing that urge to speak. Use your faith to sense that urge, that "want to", that desire.

You will sense that urge by faith, no matter how faint it is. Now that you have sensed that urge, your own will kicks in — will you believe God's Word or will you yield to traditions? Typically, your will kicks in to resist that urge to say syllables which don't sound like your everyday language. You should begin to give voice to that urge by speaking it out. Instead of resisting, you should decide to let go. Choose to relax instead of being tense. You already believe. Decide that whatever happens, you will not be silent, quiet or voiceless. As a continuous expression of your faith, decide not to speak any language that you already know.

In most cases, the urge to speak is accompanied by increased pressure on your tongue. Words appear to just rise up to your tongue even though you are not thinking about them. As an exception, some people see or hear these sounds rising from inside.

Continue to speak these new syllables, no matter the threats that your brain is sending your way. You are not foolish, crazy, mad nor have you lost your mind. You are setting your will to speak out what you believe. Remember that the Holy Ghost is not going to speak, you are.

Said more positively, you are receiving a gift and you are choosing to express that gift by speaking words in a relaxed attitude without any tension. Zero in on those two things – YOU are receiving and YOU are speaking. All else is unimportant.

When you speak in tongues, your spirit is talking. The Holy Spirit is educating your spirit. Your spirit will understand the revelation that the Holy Spirit brings as you speak in tongues. As you read the bible and keep speaking in tongues, the cumulative effect is that your spirit will reveal that truth to your natural mind. The more you allow your spirit practice this, your spirit matures through this process of learning and the thoughts of your spiritual mind become more mature. Your mind starts knowing things it did not know before. The mysteries are becoming knowledge to your mind.

9

Stammering Lips

If you find yourself repeating the same set of syllables over and over when you speak in tongues, should you keep things that way?

And the very God of peace sanctify you wholly; and I pray God your whole spirit and soul and body be preserved blameless unto the coming of our Lord Jesus Christ.

[1 THESSALONIANS 5:23]

Language is giving sounds to objects and having others agree with you that the sound refers to those objects in a fixed way. This then forms part of our understanding. If I walked up to a Chinese man and had him repeat an Arabic word after me, he might succeed in repeating the Arabic sound, which would have a meaning to an Arab but not to that Chinese man. His mind would be uncomfortable with that experience since he would not know if he just agreed to sign away all his wealth to me. What he is saying is a mystery to his mind, though it is not a mystery to the Arab.

What would happen, if you were transported back in time and you were tasked with explaining Facebook messaging to your ancestors who lived one thousand years ago? Even if you shared the same language with that ancestor, in order to explain the phenomena to your ancestor all the words that you use would be new words as far as your ancestor is concerned. In that illustration, your ancestor is your soul and you who are aware of Facebook chat, is your spirit. Your spirit is far more enlightened and advanced than your soul and it has words, sentences and phrases that your soul does not grasp. This is speaking in tongues.

All believers are spirit beings; by extension all believers can and should let their spirits pray. The question is not one of whether all can pray in tongues but rather, "are all spirits"? If so, does the spirit voice out itself in prayer? When the spirit voices itself in prayer, what would it sound like? Paul gives us the answer in 1 Corinthians 14. When your spirit prays it will flow out as tongues (1 Cor. 14:14). Thus we don't pray in tongues because we are Pentecostals but because we are spirit beings who recognize that our spirits have a voice.

Tongues involves spirit, soul & body

Speaking in tongues involves the whole man – the spirit, the soul and the body. Your human spirit is the one doing the speaking while your soul is making choices on a moment-by-moment basis. It is not your emotion or your mind but your will that is involved in initiating speaking in tongues. The body is yielding to the will of man as the will takes control of the mouth, vocal chords and the tongue. Speaking in tongues leaves the human will intact. It is demons that try to force or coerce, God does not. When we speak in tongues we are using our lips, tongues and vocal chords to push sounds out of our mouth, while we voluntarily take control away from our own intellect. Speaking in tongues is not involuntary. It is deliberate yielding to God.

Since speaking in tongues is an act of the will and the will can yield in degrees. The degree of yielding by the one speaking in tongues varies. God is equally available to all, but we do not all yield to the same degree. Some people are so tense when attempting to speak in tongues that their very tension robs them of responding to the flow of the spirit. This is why some people stammer while others actually speak.

> *In the law it is written, With men of other tongues and other lips will I speak unto this people; and yet for all that will they not hear me, saith the Lord.*
>
> ## [1 CORINTHIANS 14:21]

Speaking in tongues is regulated by God's Word and not by our emotions or feelings. Paul's appeal to Isaiah's prophecy fixes for us the meaning of this passage in Isaiah.

> *For with stammering lips and another tongue will he speak to this people.*
>
> ## [ISAIAH 28:11]

Isaiah the Prophet had prophesied concerning the supernatural operation called speaking in tongues. He mentioned stammering lips as well as other tongues. He implied that one can stammer in tongues as well as speak in tongues. The basic level of speaking in tongues is stammering. It is a measure of the degree of yieldedness to God. The stammerer is trying to say something though he might not be as fluent as the non-stammerer but stammering does not make one an impostor or a fake. Just as some people's speech is smoother and clearer than that of others, we should not be surprised to find that some genuine folks stammer more in tongues than other people, and that does not make their experience any less supernatural. If there were absolutely no possibility of stammering in tongues, the Lord would not have moved upon Isaiah to prophesy it.

Stammering is the Launchpad

By putting stammering lips at the top of Isaiah's list before mentioning other tongues, God shows us that there is progression in spiritual utterances. A valid starting point could be stammering before one arrives at fully articulated language in tongues. In the natural, we speak more fluently with practice. We also get more fluent in tongues with use. By extension, a person who seldom speaks in tongues might find that he stammers in tongues more than necessary because of insufficient exercise. The prime reason why a majority of believers continue to stammer in tongues is because they are not yielding enough for a wider vocabulary to flow through. It is not mandatory to stammer in tongues but even if like most people you were to start there, keep practicing and with your mastery you will gain confidence in clearer articulation.

> *For if I pray in an unknown tongue, my spirit prayeth, but my understanding is unfruitful. 15 What is it then? I will pray with the spirit, and I will pray with the understanding also: I will sing with the spirit, and I will sing with the understanding also.*
>
> [1 CORINTHIANS 14:15]

When we speak in our everyday vernacular, our wills are involved. The same will is involved when we speak in tongues. Every person who speaks in tongues is multi-lingual. A multi-lingual person would make choices concerning which language they want to express themselves in. It is our wills that choose how frequently we speak in tongues.

> *To whom he said, This is the rest wherewith ye may cause the weary to rest; and this is the refreshing: yet they would not hear.*
>
> [ISAIAH 28:12]

Speaking or stammering in tongues is the rest that dismantles weariness. There is a rest that we absorb from speaking in tongues that is not available through any other means. This rest is primarily spiritual. The effect of spiritual rest is more long lasting than physical rest. Spiritual rest will slowly seep into your cellular makeup and bring calm to your chemical constitution and your emotions. There are many Christians who try to use medication to fall asleep because their bodies find it difficult to drift into sleep. I usually encourage people to first rest spiritually through speaking in tongues, and then allow their bodies absorb that rest before they rest their bodies at night in sleep. If you believe that you get a rest and refreshing from speaking in tongues you will experience it faster. If however, you do not have understanding in this area, you will be unable to maximize the rest that is supplied when you pray in tongues.

Increase your vocabulary in tongues

Even in the case of inanimate objects which are capable of making sound, such as a flute or harp, if their notes all sound alike, who can tell what tune is being played? Unless the bugle-note is clear who will be called to arms? There are in the world a great variety of spoken sounds and each has a distinct meaning.

[1 CORINTHIANS 14:8,10 - PHILLIPS]

When we speak in tongues, we are speaking a real language. Each sound has a specific meaning. In our everyday conversations, we get better as we say enough sounds to convey complete meaning. When there are no sounds, there is no meaning. This is true of any language. It is also true of tongues.

If a spirit-filled believer keeps repeating the same syllables when speaking in tongues, he is repeating the same sounds and ideas in the spirit. Just as with any language, each sound behind those spiritual utterances has specific meaning. A believer that simply repeats the same sounds over and over again is saying the same thing over and over again in the spirit. I would rather a man repeats himself in tongues than abandon speaking in tongues altogether. If we have limited vocabulary in tongues, we are only saying very little, therefore we are hindered from being more effective in prayer. Speaking in tongues is not magical. It is not based on what you think but what you actually say. You cannot be said to have spoken out something that you have not really said. This means that it is in the best interest of the person talking in tongues to mature until there is a wider set of sounds when speaking in tongues. Each sound has its signification or meaning. Therefore, more vocabulary carries more meaning and gets more done spiritually. A toddler trying to convey what he wants done is not quite as effective as an adult who is a brilliant communicator with a wider vocabulary. It is the same in the spirit.

The new-born babe in Christ has limited range in tongues just like babies in the natural. The baby must grow as it feeds on God's Word and learns to yield further to the Holy Ghost (1 Pet 2:2). It is not God's plan for any believer to remain a baby with a stunted prayer language. It is also not in the believer's best interest. Stammering (and limited vocabulary) in tongues means we are not fully conveying as much as we can convey. We should desire to become better in our articulation in tongues. We do not have to remain infants in these things. When the Holy Spirit operates tongues for intercession through a believer, if the believer repeats over and again the same few syllables in tongues, that believer should be praised for his obedience to pray. Not many believers make themselves available today. However, that believer would not be as effective as he should have been. His limited vocabulary means he is not covering as much grounds as he would have if he had progressed further in other tongues.

10

The Diversities of Tongues

When they heard this, they were baptized in the name of the Lord Jesus. And when Paul had laid his hands upon them, the Holy Ghost came on them; and they spake with tongues, and prophesied. And all the men were about twelve.

[ACTS 19:5-7]

After Paul laid hands on this group at Ephesus they spoke in tongues and prophesied. We do not know how many women and children were in that group but we do know there were twelve men. At least twelve believers were speaking publicly in tongues at once without anyone making a fuss about what they were doing. Paul did not think anything was amiss.

As far as we can tell, there was no interpretation. Paul did not make any attempt to stop them. This practice of twelve people speaking out in tongues all at once is valid.

Does the Corinthian Instruction agree with the practice in Ephesus?

If any man speak in an unknown tongue, let it be by two, or at the most by three, and that by course; and let one interpret.

[1 CORINTHIANS 14:27]

Paul said to the Corinthians that it should be "two or at the most three". He also instructed that if there be no interpreter, people should keep quiet and speak to themselves and to God. Was Paul wrong, when he allowed more than twelve people speak in tongues at once in Ephesus? Was Peter wrong when he allowed the household of Cornelius speak in tongues all at once (Acts 10:46)? Did Paul practice his own instructions?

Since Paul did not stop those twelve from all speaking at once, that expression must be valid when all who are present speak in tongues. There is therefore, a valid exercise of speaking in tongues that allows twelve believers to speak out publicly at once. This valid expression is not to be forbidden. In that instance, no one interprets what anyone is saying in tongues. This makes sense if whatever was being said was between each speaker and God and not for the consumption of others who were present.

This is quite different from the requirement to have "two or three" while one interprets. The reason for interpretation in that instance is that what has been spoken in tongues is relevant to those present. This whole Church would then understand what has been said in tongues.

If we don't come to a similar conclusion, we find ourselves arguing that Paul changed his mind between Ephesus and Corinth! Worse still, we think Paul enforced one set of rules at Corinth while letting the

Ephesians do as they well pleased. I believe that these records in the bible force us to renew our minds. It is not that Paul changed his mind but that the scope covered by the instructions on interpretation of tongues is different from what happened at Ephesus. Thus there are two broad expressions of the exercise of speaking in tongues. One expression requires public interpretation while the other does not. This means that there are varieties and diversities, when it comes to tongues and it is not one rule that regulates all.

One rule does not fit all

All tongues are essentially the same; the difference is in its purpose. We must seek to understand the purpose as well as the correct way for exercising speaking in tongues. When the tongue spoken is addressed to the people present, there is a need for interpretation. At Ephesus, they did not exercise tongues that required interpretation, therefore no one interpreted. The tongues were between the speaker and God, so it wasn't to be interpreted for the benefit of the whole assembly.

Since Paul gave instructions that two or three should speak in tongues, he implies that more than three people might feel that they have a message in tongues in a service for those present to listen to and be blessed by. In those circumstances, the people are not speaking in tongues of the sort that those twelve spoke in at Ephesus. They have a message from God to the Church. Therefore, whatever they say in tongues should be followed by interpretation. Interestingly, since he also said one should interpret the tongues, this means that in a spirit-filled church more than one person might feel that they have the interpretation of that which was spoken in tongues. In those instances, Paul says not to allow everyone have a go at giving their interpretation. It should be one person doing the interpreting.

There is no confusion once we understand that it is not a one-rule-fits-all scenario and that there are tongues not to be interpreted as well as tongues to be interpreted.

Gifts, administrations and operations

Now there are diversities of gifts, but the same Spirit. And there are differences of administrations, but the same Lord. And there are diversities of operations, but it is the same God which worketh all in all.

[1 CORINTHIANS 12:4-6]

This chapter discusses more than the gifts of the Spirit. Paul is discussing three distinct things – gifts, administrations and operations.

The Holy Spirit places the gifts within the church for the profiting of all members of the body of Christ. Administrations are not the same thing as the nine gifts of the Spirit. Administrations refer to the various offices in the body of Christ. It is the Lord Jesus that is directly responsible for all the offices. He places these administrations or offices in the body of Christ. In respect to operations, we see that the Father then works all in all. This means that the Father God works all of the gifts into all the offices. This is why certain gifts are more pronounced in certain offices. It is also why people who stand in similar offices tend to express the call in different ways.

Entry level for all members

Now ye are the body of Christ, and members in particular. 28 And God hath set some in the church, first apostles, secondarily prophets, thirdly teachers, after that miracles, then gifts of healings, helps, governments, diversities of tongues.

[1 CORINTHIANS 12:27-28]

The Church is not the building where we hold our fellowship meetings. When we leave the building, some other people could lease it for a conference, a birthday party or some other public or private use. The building remains the same; its address does not change even though the believers have left. The building first housed the Church, and then later housed the birthday party but the building was neither a Church nor a party. The building was neither spiritual nor unspiritual, nor does it hold any particular status before God. It is simply a location on the earth, where saints meet together.

On the other hand, the universal Church is not a physical building. In fact, it is impossible to point it out from a natural standpoint, since it is a reference to every born again person, no matter where they are located on the earth or in heaven (Eph. 3:15, Col. 1:18). During this age, the universal Church cannot meet at any one location since some of its members are or earth and others are in heaven. When the members of the universal Church express themselves in a location, you have what's called the local church. The Local Church is how you fellowship with other believers in your area (Col. 1:2, Eph. 1:1, Rom. 1:7).

The word that is translated as "church" is from a Greek word that means those who have responded to the call. They received the call only because there was a call to respond to in the first place. The Church receives and responds to the call, while the Lord Jesus, as the Head of the Church, and the Father God are the ones doing the calling since they set us in the Church (Gal. 1:1).

Paul is discussing the place that each member of the body holds. He presents a list of offices within the body of Christ at the top of which we have the Apostles. Every time Apostles and Prophets are mentioned in the New Testament, they are always presented in the order of Apostles first and afterwards Prophets and never in the reverse order. It is because Paul is implying some form of ranking that he uses the words firstly, secondarily and thirdly. Everything he mentions on that list refers to people who stand in offices as a result of a call.

Apostles, Prophets and Teachers are people anointed by the Lord Jesus to minister to His body, the Church (Eph. 4:11). "Miracles" does not refer to the gifts of the Spirit but to people. Ministers of the gospel like William Braham and Kathryn Johanna Kuhlman also had this office of miracles. It is also part of an Evangelist's office.

Ministering edification to yourself

This list in 1 Cor. 12:28 helps us see that the entry into all the ministries of the Spirit, as well as all the offices that the Lord Jesus has for members of the church, is the diversities of tongues. Speaking in tongues is the signature of this Church age. Prior to the age of the Church, there was nothing like it.

The basic ministry we enter into after the New Birth is the ministry of personal edification through speaking in other tongues (1 Cor. 14:4). Some believers think that God has ordained that the primary edification the believer gets will be through exposure to the five-fold ministry gifts. They think that their edification is within these ministers. This is not God's plan at all. We hold the five-fold ministers that God has put in our lives in the uttermost esteem because God has put them in our lives to perfect (or mature) us (Eph. 4:12). These ministers see to our maturity, while we remain responsible for our personal edification.

You are the primary minister of edification into your own life. You cannot entrust this to someone else. Speaking in tongues is one avenue by which God guarantees that you get edified whenever you want to whether your Pastor is present or not. The Pastor, Teacher or Prophet is not always present but the Holy Ghost is! It is as we speak in tongues that the knowing builds within to such a degree until we know exactly where we fit in the body of Christ, otherwise we do what most people do – we stumble into any role where we see a need. A day-old believer should speak in tongues since this is the entry into spiritual things but that same day-old Christian no matter how sure he is must not step into the role of Apostle, Pastor or the ministry gifts from day one as a believer!

Since speaking in tongues is the entry, you'll find that almost anyone that says tongues are not for today will also shy away from the other manifestations of the Spirit – they have disqualified themselves by not starting in the lower room of speaking in tongues. It is as we submit ourselves to this basic gift of the Spirit that we enter fully into God's call upon our lives. There are also specialized ministries that God has equipped to minister to the saints by tongues and interpretation. When this ministry is in demonstration, the tongues tend to be of a higher quality and are accompanied with a tangibly greater anointing. For now, we are emphasizing the fact that every spirit filled believer starts at and enters in through the door of diversities of tongues.

Through the operation called the diversities of tongues, it is God's plan that you branch into anything and everything that God has in His plan for you including standing in your proper office in the body. You don't come into the body of Christ through diversities of tongues but through the New Birth. Once born again, you are to be spirit-filled so you can receive tremendous edification, which helps you recognize and fulfill your place in the body of Christ.

Speaking in tongues is a diversity

And God hath set some in the church, ... then diversities of tongues.

[1 CORINTHIANS 12:28]

The Apostle Paul was used by God to give detailed instruction about the operation of tongues in the church age. He does not just speak of tongues but of diversities of tongues. The implication is that if you try to force the same rules on the different operations of tongues without making room for their diversity, you will be hopelessly confused and that is exactly what the devil wants. The plain teaching of scriptures is that there are different operations of the diversities of tongues and we should endeavor to understand them, so as to draw maximum benefit for ourselves as well as the Church of the Lord Jesus.

There are nine manifestations of the Holy Spirit. One of the nine manifestations is what we know as the diversities of tongues. The diversities of tongues has four main branches. Three out of those four branches of diversities of tongues just like the other eight manifestations are not directly under the control of the spirit-filled believer. Thus you could say that eight and three quarter gifts are not directly under our control.

One of the four diversities of tongues is the most fundamental expression of it. It is this expression that we refer to as the basic operation of diversities of tongues. This operation of diversities of tongues for personal edification is one of the four branches. This manifestation of the spirit is definitely within our control. This basic operation is the doorway to the expression of the remaining eight and three-quarter gifts.

Let's find out about the four operations of the diversities of tongues.

The basic operation of diversity of tongues

He that speaketh in an unknown tongue edifieth himself;

[1 CORINTHIANS 14:4A]

What is it then? I will pray with the spirit, and I will pray with the understanding also: I will sing with the spirit, and I will sing with the understanding also.

[1 CORINTHIANS 14:15]

Since Paul said, "I will ..." a key characteristic of this basic diversity of tongues is the prominent part played by the will of the person speaking in tongues. You don't speak in the basic diversities of tongues as the Spirit wills but as you will. In expressing this basic diversity of tongue, it is the will of God that the spirit-filled believer sets his own will in order to speak in tongues. It is God's will that the will of man govern this operation. This is the only operation of diversity of tongues that God has given completely to man to control. Its benefit is directed towards the one speaking it.

God has yielded the control of this basic operation of tongues for private edification to the Spirit-filled believer. It is the office that all Spirit-filled believers start in and never graduate out of. This operation is not twisting God's arm nor does it make God do anything. It does not even make God lead us. All that we receive as a result of operating this basic diversity like guidance, insight, wisdom, edification and revelation are already provided for by God through Christ Jesus, whether or not we operate in diversities of tongues for edification but operating this diversity awakens us to grasp the available guidance and wisdom of God!

Remember that since God has yielded control to the speaker, you are to speak this basic diversity of tongues anytime that 'you will to'. God has graciously given you total control of the degree of edification in your life. You are the minister of edification into your own personal life.

This basic operation is the first room you enter into before the door to the other rooms open up to you. You operate this particular diversity of tongues for personal edification and praise anytime you will to until you are separated into the other operations possible within that diversity. The basic operation of diversities of tongues is for personal edification and magnifying God. All spirit-filled believers exercise this basic operation of tongues. It affects the spirit of the one speaking until the speaker diversifies into everything that is in God's plan for that person. It is on top of this basic diversity that all other operations of God in the believer's life are built. In simple language, asides from feeding on the Word, exercising this basic diversity is the place to start, if you do not know where to start. When you do not know what to do, this is what to do. If you start out with this basic operation, you will ultimately get into anything that God has in mind for you.

The basic operation of tongues for building up myself (as a believer) and magnifying God can be engaged as often and as long as I am willing. It is not up to God because He has left its operation completely in my stewardship to use as frequently and as long as I choose to.

You will find out in your practice of the Word that the overwhelming majority of time you'd spend speaking, singing and praying in tongues will be outside a church service. If all your tongue talking is in a church service, you are a baby Christian still on skimmed milk!

This basic operation of the diversities of tongues awakens the anointing within you for your personal benefit to teach you all things from the mind of Christ (1 Cor. 2:7). Through this teaching, you are guided into divine wisdom and all truth. Speaking in tongues through this particular operation is the bucket that we dip into the river of revelation and guidance. Speaking in tongues as an exercise of the basic operation of diversity of tongues is a primary means of obtaining edification.

Edification, what is it?

> He that speaketh in an unknown tongue edifieth himself; but he that prophesieth edifieth the church.
>
> [1 CORINTHIANS 14:4]

One definite thing about when you talk in tongues is that you are talking to God and mysteries are being communicated. God is not getting mysteries from you, you are the one getting mysteries from Him.

Edification requires that you already have the Word of God in you richly. Speaking in tongues does not give you the Word; it gives you the weapons to dislodge the grip of wrong interpretations and wrong thinking regarding the Word; but it does not get into the Word for you. This edification is separating and stripping us from the power of false thoughts, imagination and beliefs that weigh us down. It is a download of insight in areas where we had been ignorant. It is as we submit to the teacher within, as we speak in tongues that we are stripped of ignorance of the unknown. This is the primary edification of tongues. Speaking in tongues is more than just a mechanism for receiving edification; it is a door into the world of revelation.

The believer, though complete from the perspective of the spirit man, is still open to deception and false beliefs. It is our soul that accepts these false doctrines and practices. All the while, our spirit knows that our soul is really being a dummy. The edification received while speaking in tongues causes the soul to be delivered from its dummy acts. Edification causes you to stop trying to get what is already yours because you find it more commonsensical to reason from your spiritual mind. Edification is not the product of five minutes speaking in tongues. Real edification is cumulative and it affects the soul over a long period. It might take your soul a while to get there but if you keep at it, edification will set you on the journey from deception to freedom.

Usually, no matter how spiritually insensitive or carnal the believer may be, and no matter what valley the believer finds himself in, the Spirit-filled believer can operate the basic diversities of tongues for personal edification and magnifying God. This point is important. Operating this basic diversity of tongues will supply the edification to elevate and promote you above any mess (Jude 20).

This operation of diversity of tongues is private and is not usually interpreted in a verbal way as you would the diversities of tongues for public edification, though you can expect God to give you insight. Your spirit still picks up the facts concerning what you have spoken in tongues. It will be a function of spiritual growth. You can desire to interpret your private tongues. You don't arrive there by praying 10 minutes in tongues daily. The benefits of speaking in tongues become more obvious only as you spend longer times praying in tongues daily.

> *Which things also we speak, not in the words which man's wisdom teacheth, but which the Holy Ghost teacheth; comparing spiritual things with spiritual.*
>
> ### [1 CORINTHIANS 2:13]

The basic operation of tongues is the language that the Holy Ghost teaches. This language is like a bucket that draws substance from the river of God's wisdom. We understand this wisdom with the mind of Christ, which we receive at the new birth. This works by comparing the spiritual things of the reborn spirit with the spiritual things of God's divine nature to draw upon wisdom and insight. The basic operation of diversities of tongues is therefore a personal revelation gift for your own benefit to enrich your spiritual walk.

And when Paul had laid his hands upon them, the Holy Ghost came on them; and they spake with tongues, and prophesied.

[ACTS 19:6]

As is often the case, when people start exercising themselves in the basic operation of diversities of tongues for personal edification, they get edified to the point where something is triggered within their spirits to start yielding to other operations of the Holy Spirit. People often start prophesying immediately afterwards. Even in the bible, it is fairly obvious that prophecy tends to follow speaking in tongues. This prophecy is not the interpretation of tongues but a separate gift of the spirit.

This basic operation of tongues in the private life is the primary way that the Holy Spirit brings revelation knowledge into your life. We humans think in pictures and not in words. When I say "car", I don't see the letters C-A-R. What I see is the mental image of a motorcar. In the same way, these Spirit-inspired words that we utter in tongues, like any kind of spoken words paint pictures that our spirits then project upon our understanding. Over a long period, this builds our understanding. It becomes a clear outline. It builds an inner vision and sharpens our spiritual sense of seeing and knowing. The more you exercise yourself in this basic operation, the sharper your spiritual perception. It is not up to the Holy Ghost, it is up to you. He is always ready; you are the one that switches on and off.

The operation of diverse tongues for edifying others

The second operation of diversities of tongues is the operation of diversities of tongues for the edification of others.

There are some who argue against the existence of this operation. It is obvious from 1 Corinthians 14:21 which says "In the law it is written, With men of other tongues and other lips will I speak unto this people …" that speaking in tongues is not always a case of man speaking to God. Since tongues is the signature of this Church age, I expect that in the Church age, God has a lot that He wants to say to His people through other tongues.

> *I would that ye all spake with tongues but rather that ye prophesied: for greater is he that prophesieth than he that speaketh with tongues, except he interpret, that the church may receive edifying. If any man speak in an unknown tongue, let it be by two, or at the most by three, and that by course; and let one interpret.*

[1 CORINTHIANS 14:5, 27]

Usually, when a person's voice is raised over and above the general noise level in the congregation, it should indicate that the person has something to say that the whole church needs to hear. This is not often the case. A person who is speaking the basic diversities of tongues should not raise their voice above everyone else, for it will attract unnecessary attention.

This operation of the diversity of tongues is not the same as the basic operation for personal edification. This diversity is for the edification of others and unlike the basic operation of diversities of tongues, this operation must always be interpreted. The operation of diverse tongues for edifying others is therefore always followed by another related gift, the interpretation of tongues. This interpretation is not just a function of spiritual growth; it is an anointing of God's Spirit coming upon the one who is used in public interpretation of tongues.

This diversity of tongues for edifying others is not the starting point but a flow that comes about because the spirit-filled believer already operates in the building up and personal edification of their spirit man. Through this operation, God is communing with the Church through the operation of diversity of tongues. We are not directly in control of this operation, as we are in control of the other basic operation of diversities of tongues for personal edification. You cannot exercise this operation just because you want to.

If you persist in the basic operation of tongues for personal edification and praise, you'd soon find yourself being used in this diversity that requires interpretation for the benefit of the others who are present. You could say that the basic operation is private communion between God and man, while this other operation is not man towards God but God towards man. It is God speaking to man after the tongue has been interpreted.

The operation of diverse tongues for supernatural intercession

The third operation of diversities of tongues is the operation of diversities of tongues, which prays out the intercession of Jesus. This operation is initiated by the Lord Jesus, who through the Holy Ghost impresses our hearts to pray. Like the basic operation for edification, this diversity of tongue also operates in the private life of the believer.

This operation of the diversity of tongues for praying out the will of God for others, is linked with the High Priesthood of Jesus (Heb. 7:25). While the Lord Jesus is in the heavens at the right hand of God, He cannot legally directly pray for humans on the earth (Ezek. 22:30, Ps. 115:16). This is why we don't find Him laying hands on anyone for healing or going about preaching after He rose from the dead. The Lord Jesus transfers the prayer aspects of His intercession to our spirits, by the Holy Ghost, for us to pray out on the earth (John 16:14, Rom. 8:27). Under the anointing, this is sometimes accompanied with groaning.

At different times, different believers have seen this diversity of tongues in operation and have themselves been used by God in the operation of this diversities of tongues. They assume that this operation is within their control because they mistake this for the rules that govern the operation of tongues for personal edification and magnifying God. They therefore get into all sorts of excesses trying to conjure up various actions and sounds. Some folks stir up their flesh to roar like lions, others groan like a woman in childbirth, some bark like a dog and some others fly like a bird and all sort of weirdness because they fail to see that this operation is not under our control.

This operation of the diversity of tongues for praying out the intercession of Jesus for others in its true expression might not be spectacular but it is supernatural. As we learn to maintain a spirit filled life, we will flow in this diversity unconsciously in our prayer life. This way of praying is the product of firstly exercising oneself in the basic diversities of tongues for personal edification in our private lives. The relationship between the basic operations and the exercise of this particular diversity is illustrated in Jude.

> *But ye, beloved, building up yourselves on your most holy faith, praying in the Holy Ghost, Keep yourselves in the love of God, looking for the mercy of our Lord Jesus Christ unto eternal life. And of some have compassion, making a difference:*
>
> [JUDE 20 - 22]

As you exercise the basic operation of diversities of tongues for personal edification and magnifying God, you are actually building yourself up to locate your most holy faith, which is the faith of Christ within you. As you persist in that basic operation, you keep yourself within the love of God. It is as you keep yourself in the love of God that the compassion of God grips your heart so it becomes tenderer. It is from this tender heart that we lend ourselves to the diversities of tongues for praying out the intercession of Jesus. The Lord Jesus by the Holy Spirit pours out His intercession through you. It is not where you start out but often where we end up under the direction of the Holy Ghost.

This operation of the diversity of tongues for praying out the will of God for others in cooperation with the Lord Jesus is not directly under our control but only indirectly, as we first give ourselves extensively to the basic operation of building up ourselves above the mess of the flesh and sensuality.

The operation of diverse tongues as a sign

The fourth operation of diversities of tongues is the operation of diversities of tongues, which operates as a sign.

This operation of the diversity of tongues as a sign is not the same thing as a Spirit-filled believer speaking the basic operation of tongues for edification and magnifying God in the presence of the unsaved. If you operate the basic tongues for personal edification for the unsaved to hear, its purpose is still to edify you personally. The fact that you happen to be speaking in tongues in the presence of an unbeliever does not mean it is a sign to that unbeliever (except of course it is a sign to that unbeliever that you are a nut case (1 Cor. 14:23)); nor does it direct the tongues at the unbeliever. You are still having a conversation between your human spirit and God's spirit and triggering the rules for your spiritual edification. Speaking in tongues in the presence of a sinner is not the fourth valid operation of diversities of tongues. That's just an attention seeker who is not instructed in the proper exercise of tongues.

> *Wherefore tongues are for a sign, not to them that believe, but to them that believe not: but prophesying serveth not for them that believe not, but for them which believe.*
>
> [1 CORINTHIANS 14:22]

There are some who argue that in the bible, every recorded instance of tongues occurred in the presence of an unsaved Jew. Therefore, according to them, we can only have a valid expression of speaking in tongues when an unsaved Jew is present! Firstly, the bible does not say that tongues were a sign specifically to the unsaved Jew, but to "them that believe not". This is true whether the one that believes not is a Jew or a non-Jew. Furthermore, it is simply not true that speaking in tongues only occurred when an unsaved Jew was present.

When Paul went to Ephesus those present were either part of Paul's missionary team or the Ephesian group consisting of twelve men besides women and children (Acts 17:6). After these disciples became Christians, Paul laid hands on them and they spoke in tongues as well as prophesied. By the time these new Christians began to speak in tongues, everyone in that setting was a Christian. Paul did not at first tell these new converts to hold their peace until he could find an unsaved Jew from the street who would receive the tongues spoken as a sign before these believers could speak in tongues. That borders on the ridiculous.

> *While Peter yet spake these words, the Holy Ghost fell on all them which heard the word. And they of the circumcision which believed were astonished, as many as came with Peter, because that on the Gentiles also was poured out the gift of the Holy Ghost. For they heard them speak with tongues, and magnify God. Then answered Peter,*

[ACTS 10:44-46]

We have another scenario of tongues in Cornelius' house. When Peter got to that house, he and six Jewish brethren that came with him were Christians, while Cornelius and his family were not. Peter was still preaching when the Holy Ghost fell on all them that heard the Word. Given that the six people that came with Peter were Christian Jews and that all who heard the Word in Cornelius house became Christians, it means that by the time Cornelius and his crew were speaking in tongues, there was no unsaved Jew or unsaved Gentile in that room. We don't find Peter berating everyone for speaking in tongues all at once because there were no unsaved Jews in the room.

The Holy Ghost did not have such qualms and Peter quickly agreed with what he recognized as the handiwork of God. So we see that neither Paul nor Peter nor the Holy Ghost had any qualms about Christians speaking in tongues when there is no unsaved Jew around to receive it as a sign.

There is however a genuine operation of diversities of tongues as a sign to the one who does not believe.

Some examples of tongues as a sign

We are back at Cornelius' house.

> *While Peter yet spake these words, the Holy Ghost fell on all them which heard the word. And they of the circumcision which believed were astonished, as many as came with Peter, because that on the Gentiles also was poured out the gift of the Holy Ghost. For they heard them speak with tongues, and magnify God. Then answered Peter, Can any man forbid water, that these should not be baptized, which have received the Holy Ghost as well as we?*

[ACTS 10:44-47]

We know something significant has happened because of the effect on the Jewish Christians – they were astonished when they heard the Gentiles speak in tongues. There is no indication that anyone exercised the gift of interpretation of tongues. This would mean that each of those Christian Jews heard the meaning of what the Gentiles were saying in tongues. This is how they could tell that the Gentiles were magnifying God. People understood the content of things spoken in tongues without anyone getting up to interpret. It convicted the Christians who were present. It set them free from prejudice. Prior to this event, the Jewish Christians did not believe that God had opened the door for the salvation of the Gentiles.

What was the purpose of this sign?

It was a sign to Peter and the Jewish party who had come with him that God was extending salvation to the Gentiles and had accepted them on equal footing into the body of Christ (Acts 11:18). It is fairly obvious that if not for this astonishing sign, those Christian Jews would not have been convinced as to the genuineness of the salvation of the Gentiles. This sign convinced the Jews that the Gentiles really could be saved without first obeying the Law of Moses. (In Acts 10 was there interpretation?)

When tongues are spoken (or heard) in a language that the sinner understands without any need for the interpretation of tongues, we have tongues as a sign to the unbeliever. The tongues spoken is still unknown to the speaker but is understood by the hearer without needing any interpretation. It is this operation that is a sign to that unbelieving one. This operation is not under the control of the Spirit-filled believer unlike the basic operation of diversities of tongues for personal edification. It is still the same tongues per se but its purpose is different. One should not seek to manufacture this operation. Well, if you try to, you'd be found out and you'll sound supremely phoney anyway!

This operation of diversities of tongues as a sign to the unbeliever was exercised on the day of Pentecost.

> *And they were all filled with the Holy Ghost, and began to speak with other tongues, as the Spirit gave them utterance. And there were dwelling at Jerusalem Jews, devout men, out of every nation under heaven. Now when this was noised abroad, the multitude came together, and were confounded, because that every man heard them speak in his own language.*
>
> [ACTS 2:4-6]

Whatever the disciples spoke, it was not Hebrew, or Aramaic or any common language of the day. If they had spoken a language common to all, no one would have been confounded!

If 120 people speak at once you'll agree it would be impossible to make out what each person was saying. Yet by some supernatural operation of God, each Jew present "heard them speak in his own language"!

There is no record of anyone stepping forward to start interpreting to the Jews who were gathered. Each Jew said they heard the Galileans speaking the wonderful works of God. They all heard at once in their various languages. Everyone present was able to pick out specifically what was being said in each of their languages even though 120 men and women were all speaking in tongues simultaneously. This operation of diversities of tongues definitely arrests the attention of the unbelievers who are present. This operation is not designed with the spirit-filled believer in mind but for the unbeliever, therefore you will not see it in operation in a believers' meeting, where all that are present are believers.

The key idea is that the operation of the diversities of tongues as a sign does not require interpretation of tongues. The intended hearer instantly understands it.

I once heard of an instance, where this operation of the diversities of tongues was a sign was in operation. It was in a meeting in Florida where a certain minister was teaching from a portion of Romans 8. This Minister noticed that there were two men huddled in a corner at the back of the auditorium and one of the men whispered in the ear of the other anytime the minister made a point. The minister felt this was rude but kept ministering the Word. They seemed to talk right through until about half way through the teaching when the guys suddenly stopped talking and things remained that way till the end of the service. The minister closed the meeting and went to his hotel.

The host pastor later called his attention to the two men that kept whispering to each other through most of the service and asked if the minister knew why they suddenly stopped talking during the service. The minister felt it was because they discovered that their action was irreverent. The Pastor then informed this visiting minister that one of the men was a French speaking gentleman who did not speak any English but wanted to come for those set of meetings, so he brought along his own personal interpreter who was interpreting the message to the French gentleman as the minister taught. The minister now understood what had been going on but then got more puzzled wondering why the men stopped talking mid-way through the service. Had the minister said something to offend both men so they no longer felt a need to continue to discuss what the minister was teaching?

The Pastor responded that the men came to her excitedly after the meeting to let her know that the French gentleman was deeply impressed when the minister stopped ministering in English halfway through the service and switched to supplying instruction to them in pure French! It was because the minister switched to French that the gentleman told his interpreter there was no more need for interpretation as he could now hear the minister in his native French. Interestingly, the host Pastor did not hear the minister teach in French at any time during the service. None of the other members of the congregation heard the minister teach in French and in fact the recording confirmed that the minister had spoken all through in English. When these two French-speaking guys were questioned as to what they heard in French, it turns out that the two men had heard exactly what every other member of the congregation had heard in English! Somehow,, the Holy Spirit had interpreted what the minister was saying in English and caused those two men to hear it in French. This was a modification of the day of Pentecost. The minister was not even aware there was an operation of any diversity of tongues, but the effect on those two French men was just as if the man had switched over to another Language.

11

Unknown Tongues in Corinthians

Now concerning spiritual gifts, brethren, I would not have you ignorant.2 Ye know that ye were Gentiles, carried away unto these dumb idols, even as ye were led.3 Wherefore I give you to understand, that no man speaking by the Spirit of God calleth Jesus accursed: and that no man can say that Jesus is the Lord, but by the Holy Ghost.4 Now there are diversities of gifts, but the same Spirit.5 And there are differences of administrations, but the same Lord.6 And there are diversities of operations, but it is the same God which worketh all in all.7 But the manifestation of the Spirit is given to every man to profit withal.

[1 CORINTHIANS 12:1-7]

The first seven verses of 1 Corinthians 12 serve the same purpose that a table of content would serve in a modern textbook. Paul discusses some things that are gifts, others that are administrations and a third category that are operations. For the gifts that "say" something – diversities of tongues, interpretation of tongues and prophecy - the purpose is edification, exhortation and comfort.

The gift is never faulty

The gift is never faulty but the administration or stewardship of it involves the human element and that is where we improve. The operation speaks of the various combinations of each of those utterance gifts together with the administration of them. The operation of tongues and interpretation of tongues is diverse. You can operate it in your private life, sing it, chant it, speak it, use it in prayer, in praise, as well as in various operations in public life of the church, when the assembly is gathered together. It is failure to distinguish between the operations in private and public that leads to much confusion today. We should not be careless in studying what the epistles say about the exercise of speaking in tongues as well as interpretation of tongues.

Tongues and interpretation implied?

The bible contains countless examples of the exercise of prophecy as well as the exact content of various prophecies. It is noteworthy however that there are no clearly stated examples in scripture of the gift of tongues and interpretation of tongues being used together in a church service. The correction in 1 Corinthians 14 implies that tongues and interpretation definitely occurred together and were so commonplace that excesses began to creep into the church. Why examples of interpretation of tongues are not given is quite intriguing! Could it be that it is by God's design that the specific instance of the exercise of tongues and interpretation of tongues and its content are not written? Perhaps there is such diversity and richness possible in the exercise of tongues and interpretation of tongues as distinctive of the church age that had the actual examples been documented, we might restrict ourselves to those specific example seen in scripture, thus restricting the rich diversity in God's original design?

I am convinced that the more we seek to understand these things the more the questions that we will have – and that is not a bad thing!

Paul said "the Holy Ghost witnesseth in every city, saying that bonds and afflictions abide me" (Acts 20:23). This would be through the gifts that say. That's either prophecy or tongues and interpretation. Acts 19:6 specifically pointed out when people prophesied at Ephesus. Acts 21:9 also specifically mentioned Phillip's daughters who prophesied. It is my opinion that since it does not specifically say prophecy, this witness of the Holy Ghost in every city would likely be through tongues and interpretation of tongues.

I believe that psalms, hymns and spiritual songs should be the natural outcome of about 95% of interpretation of tongues in the private life. In which case,, the tongue given is actually magnifying God and is directed from man to God. Therefore, the interpretation given would in effect be profound praise. I find that this happens frequently in my own life as a Christian. Why this is not the typical practice among Pentecostals is a riddle we must resolve. It is a primary way of letting the indwelling Holy Ghost be your personal psychologist.

The existence of Paul's corrections in 1 Corinthians 14 tells us that there is a need to continue to educate believers concerning what the correct motivation should be when delivering these powerful utterance gifts. We need steady instruction in the proper use of the utterance gifts of the spirit. There was excess, confusion and disorder in Paul's day and there will likely be in our day. We should follow the pattern set by the Spirit and get believers grounded in the meaning of those instructions as well as the thinking behind them.

Keep practicing

The misuse of tongues and interpretation of tongues will lead to confusion and disorder. That possibility should not cause us to shy away from practice but should spur us on to understand their uses as well as gaining scriptural insight into how to administer them. If we find ourselves censoring believers from speaking in tongues, we will also find that we are hindering believers from getting those specific needs that are best met by the exercise of tongues in both the private and public life of the church. We definitely have as much need of tongues as the early church and as the old timers but why is there a marked decrease in the expression of these gifts today? The singular reason is that there is far less teaching on spiritual gifts than there used to be in the past. Some folks live in that misguided opinion that they are enlightened beyond the need to exercise themselves continuously in the edification that flows from speaking in tongues. We should aim for a return to a proper use of the gift of speaking in tongues so that we reap the original intent of the Spirit.

There was abuse of the utterance gifts in Corinth. The Spirit still endorsed the continued exercise of the gifts and definitely instructed Paul to write, "forbid not to speak with tongues". Paul also gives regulations about its exercise in the assembly. The mere fact that he gave instruction about the proper use while not giving such regulation about the six other manifestations of the spirit, tells us that the utterance gifts of the spirit should be so pronounced in this church age that regulations will be required about how to administer it.

Diverse kinds of tongues

When 1 Corinthians 12:10 states, "to another divers kinds of tongues;" the word translated "kinds" in kinds of tongues is the Greek word from which we get genetics. Thus it refers to species or different ethnicities. I believe that it straddles every language known to man as well as angels.

Unknown tongues

For he that speaketh in an unknown tongue speaketh not unto men, but unto God: for no man understandeth him; howbeit in the spirit he speaketh mysteries.

[1 CORINTHIANS 14:2]

This verse is commonly interpreted to be a reference to tongues in the private life, what is sometimes called "prayer language". This agrees with the phrase, "speaketh not unto men, but unto God". The direction of the speech is from man towards God and not from God towards man. It specifically says, "speaketh not unto men". Therefore, should this tongue be interpreted, I would anticipate that the interpretation would not be a message from God to man, would it? If what is spoken in tongues is a prayer, its interpretation has to be a prayer.

The expression "unknown" tongues occurred six times in chapter 14. The whole context is the exercise of tongues from the perspective of the whole church that are assembled together in one place.

This term "unknown" is italicised because it was inserted by the translators and was never part of the Greek original. Therefore, there are those who reason that since the word "unknown" is not in the Greek, there is nothing like an unknown tongue. They also say that Acts 2 shows that well over a dozen language groups were represented. These were all Jewish men who lived in different countries. Every one of those men heard "the wonderful works of God" in their own tongue. So they affirm that the tongues spoken were definitely known to those present. They insist that tongues as spoken in Acts were actually earthly languages known to the hearers who were present. This argument only makes sense if there was no gift called the interpretation of tongues. Paul argues that in the absence of the gift of interpretation of tongues, speaking in tongues to an assembly of saints would be speaking words that are not "easy to be understood" (1 Cor. 14:9). These words spoken in tongues will be like "speaking into the air" and his conclusion is, "how shall it be known what is spoken?" Putting all this together it does not make sense to insist that there is nothing like unknown tongues. The plain reading of the Corinthian passage lends itself to what we find in practice

— typically, the tongues spoken by the believer will not be "easy to be understood" and the hearers will "not know the meaning of the voice" (1 Cor. 14:11). It will be like noise to the natural ear for it is not the language of the people. While unknown is not in the Greek, the translators got it right.

Reading through the book of Acts it would appear that there are only two utterance gifts — Prophecy and Tongues. No direct mention is made of the third gift of utterance, the gift of interpretation of tongues anywhere in the book of Acts. We do not know about the existence of this gift until we get into Corinthians. The truth is that you do not properly understand the spiritual gifts that are in operation in the book of Acts until you read and renew your mind to the various instructions in Corinthians. It is not obvious from reading the Acts of Apostles alone that there was any gift that should accompany the gift of diverse kinds of tongues to complete it but Paul plainly shows that there is — it is the gift of interpretation of tongues (1 Cor. 14:5). You would not find a single mention of interpretation of tongues by name in the book of Acts. It would have been in operation but we do not know for sure until we find it in the Corinthian epistles. It is not obvious from reading the text of Acts alone that the believers speaking in tongues get edified but once you see that fact in Corinthians, you can go back to the book of Acts and pin point the effects of edification in the book of Acts.

Tongues in the public assembly

The main thrust of chapter 14 is the exercise of tongues in the presence of other believers or during a church service. Paul illustrates using a fellow who is speaking in tongues but is actually blessing with the spirit or giving thanks well. He affirms that the end product of this fellow interpreting his tongues is that the congregation will be able to say, "Amen at thy giving of thanks" (1 Cor. 14:16). Thus implying that this "blessing with the spirit" is actually using tongues for the giving of thanks. If the utterance in tongues is thanksgiving, the interpretation should not be anything other than supernatural thanksgiving flowing as a river of praise whose waters never run dry. It is every inch as supernatural as the "message" in tongues from God to His people. In fact, the case can be made that while not every saint will deliver a public message from God to the people through tongues and interpretation, almost every saint should be encouraged at some point to give an utterance in tongues followed by an interpretation that is pure praise.

Interpreting public praise

Except we take "thou givest thanks well" (1 Cor. 14:17) to be God thanking the congregation through the interpretation of tongues, we would have to agree that it is more likely that it is someone within the congregation thanking God. This would mean that he is exercising the tongues as a means of praying to God while the congregation is listening. Such praying in tongues is by the human spirit and not the human intellect. In such cases, the intellect is unfruitful therefore the intellect cannot properly say "Amen at thy giving of thanks" (Acts 14:16). This powerful prayer of thanksgiving by the Holy Ghost through the spirit of man would be an instance of blessing with the spirit. This blessing is from man to God. God would have been blessed brilliantly through the thanksgiving delivered in tongues but the congregation would not have been edified because their intellects remained unfruitful. They do not understand what has been said in tongues, which is what is meant by "seeing he understandeth not what thou sayest" (1 Cor. 14:16). He is not telling believers to shy away from giving thanks in tongues publicly. He is saying that in order to edify the whole church they should follow it up with interpretation. This makes a strong case for interpreting tongues that are not directed from God to man but from man to God in the public assembly, if the whole assembly listened to the initial tongues in the first instance. This form of thanksgiving is not widely practiced in the church today even amongst those who admit the validity of tongues and interpretation of tongues. I do not recall being in a church service where someone delivers a blessing to God in tongues and presently interpreted it. Almost all our interpretation of tongues in the public meeting comes across as a message from God to the congregation. The instruction from Paul in that scenario is that the one that delivers praise in tongues should be the one that prays for the interpretation of the tongue (1 Cor. 14:13), which would end up sounding to those present like a prayer of thanksgiving. That interpretation will bring edification, exhortation and comfort! It will most likely be expressed as psalms, hymns and spiritual songs.

People are not only edified by an interpretation of tongues when the message goes along the lines, "Oh my people ..." which would mean it is from God to man. People can also be edified listening to psalms, hymns and spiritual songs as the output of an interpretation of tongues. This should be norm in the church today.

No one understandeth

For he that speaketh in an unknown tongue speaketh not unto men, but unto God: for no man understandeth him; howbeit in the spirit he speaketh mysteries.

[1 CORINTHIANS 14:2]

When the believer speaks in tongues, his human spirit is conversing with God supernaturally. This conversation is not between the devil and the believer. We are not addressing the devil. Speaking in tongues is a means of transferring the mysteries of God into my life. We are speaking in a language that switches the speaker out of the constraints of mental comprehension and switches us into spiritual comprehension.

The challenge with some of our praying in church today is that we are supposedly talking to God but really some are lecturing others and showing off how well they can pray. The same is true of our singing. There is a place of singing to the Lord from our hearts. Even if we are weighed down by various challenges of life, our spirit still reaches out in supernatural communion to draw upon the ability of God.

There are those who are used along the lines of interpretation of tongues. These people will supernaturally understand and interpret what has been spoken in tongues. When a message has come forth in tongues and someone who is used by God in the interpretation of tongues stands up to give its interpretation, it would be incorrect to then say in such setting, "no one understandeth". The one who interprets tongues definitely understands and the people that receive that interpretation also understand. Therefore, "no one understandeth" is referring to tongues that are not to be interpreted because it is conversation flowing from the one speaking in tongues, towards the Spirit of God, as a form of spiritual communion.

Normally, if you are around other believers who are speaking in other tongues as a form of spiritual communion you would not understand. If what they are telling God is really none of your business you do not need to know. Therefore, that expression "no one understandeth", means that the purpose of this tongue is not for public interpretation. It means that the one who is speaking in tongues here is really participating in what has been aptly named "prayer language". There is no instruction to follow this through with any interpretation simply because this fellow who is speaking in his prayer language to God is enriching his communion with God as he engages in the exchange of divine secrets.

I don't know about you but I don't plan to be standing around watching another believer speak "mysteries to God" while I twiddle my thumb wondering why I don't understand what he is saying. If I were really thinking that way, I would qualify as what the bible calls "the unlearned". In the spirit of "excelling to the edifying of the church" (1 Cor. 14:12), someone should explain to me that it is a private communion between the one speaking in tongues and God. The fellow praying in tongues should then make himself less conspicuous while continuing his communion with God.

In the exercise of the gift of prophecy, God communes with the other saints present in that service through the one speaking out the words of prophecy. The mind of God is communicated to the whole assembly. Thus the communion is wider in prophecy than in unknown tongues until it is interpreted. It is because the communion encompasses a wider group in prophecy than it is through speaking in tongues that Paul prioritizes prophesying over just speaking in tongues. From the standpoint of the assembled church that are listening, they will benefit from the utterance if they understand it. The one speaking in tongues as a means of private communion to God does not need interpretation to follow it before he is blessed (1 Cor. 14:4).

Spiritual etiquette

In a setting where tongues is being exercised for private communion, the proper thing would be for the one speaking in tongues not to draw attention to himself, for there is no edification for others in that. There is a way to speak in tongues without distracting others who are present. If however, it is a prayer meeting, everyone present should be instructed to concentrate on his or her private communion with God as a means of exchanging divine secrets with God out of their spirits.

Once someone is speaking in tongues in a way that draws attention and those present start listening to that fellow flow in unknown tongues, another rule kicks in. The one flowing in unknown tongues should exercise faith that interpretation will flow forth for the benefit of the others (1 Cor. 14:13). If the one speaking in unknown tongues knows that he is actually praying to God, he can gently let everyone know that he is praying to God, seek their forgiveness for being rowdy and loud. He should then lower his voice! If you pray in unknown tongues so loudly that you grab everyone's attention, you ought to be bold enough to follow it up with interpretation. Love will see to it that they benefit from whatever it is you have been praying about. If however you are alone at home with God, you are well within your rights to burst your lungs talking to God. You'd find that you couldn't pray for extensive periods with a loud voice though. It is not that God gets nervous; it is just not sustainable for the human voice box.

"No one understandeth" does not mandate that the one speaking in tongues must not understand. There are scenarios where you should understand with your mind what you are praying out in the Spirit. The context for "No one understandeth" is that the whole Church does not understand this person's prayer language specifically because this person is talking to God and not the believers. It is private communion from the spirit of the believer to God and not about God saying anything to the assembly.

Judging tongues?

Prophecies are to be judged (1 Cor. 14:29) but there is no such instruction on judging tongues. Whereas there can be false prophecies, the bible does not cover the subject of false tongues. However, interpretation of tongues should be treated like prophecy and should therefore be judged.

Get blessed and bless others too

He that speaketh in an unknown tongue edifieth himself; but he that prophesieth edifieth the church.

[1 CORINTHIANS 14:4]

This does not teach that it is better to prophesy than to speak in tongues. If that was the case, there would be no need for God to add speaking in tongues to the church. Prophecy was already a well established and well received spiritual manifestation. What is contrasted is personal edification versus the edifying of the whole church. The setting is an assembly. Someone is speaking in what we'll call "prayer language" in private communion with the Lord in the presence of other believers. In such a case, edification is definitely generated but the whole church does not receive it. The unknown tongue was not directed at the church but at God and is between the speaker and God directly. Therefore, the edification is received by the person speaking in tongues. The inference is that the church can tell that the one speaking in tongues has received benefit without the church receiving benefit.

> *Wherefore let him that speaketh in an unknown tongue pray that he may interpret.*

[1 CORINTHIANS 14:13]

The believer mentioned here is not asking that other believers be used in the things of the Spirit though that is valid praying and there is a place for that. This believer wants to be able to edify the whole church. In context, he has spoken out something in tongues that the whole church needs interpreted. He is therefore praying a prayer that permits the one doing the praying get used further in the things of the Spirit. This speaker in an unknown tongue is now praying to function in the interpretation of tongues. This is so that he is able to minister the benefit that he has received to the whole church. In this way, the assembled saints can also benefit.

The implication is that once we speak in tongues and are edified we are also emboldened to ask for more manifestations of the spirit to be exercised through us. This instruction implies that the person speaking in tongues helps himself into further manifestations in the spirit, so that he can bring a blessing to others too. When we have the spiritual benefit of others in mind, there is no limit to what love will motivate us to ask for. Love causes us to take the spiritual initiative, with God's permission, to communicate edification to other believers who are present.

> *For if I pray in an unknown tongue, my spirit prayeth, but my understanding is unfruitful. What is it then? I will pray with the spirit, and I will pray with the understanding also: I will sing with the spirit, and I will sing with the understanding also.*

[1 CORINTHIANS 14:14-15]

Utterance in tongues does not flow from the human brain. When we speak in tongues, a mind is involved as well as a voice. The voice is man's while the mind behind the voice is God's. Thus the intellect expressed when we speak in tongues is not man's natural intellect. When we interpret tongues, the voice is wholly man's while the mind is that of the interpreter influenced by God's mind. The interpreter's mind is clearly involved since the words, idioms and style of speech of the interpreter always comes across in the interpretations. This is why no two Spirit-filled people will give exactly the same words in interpreting the same utterance in tongues though the meaning might add up to the same thing.

Since it is the human spirit doing the praying in tongues, the unknown tongues is not unknown to the spirit of the one talking in tongues. Unknown tongues is only unknown from the perspective of unfruitful understanding. The way we complete the cycle of understanding is that we will pray in tongues and subsequently pray in our understanding also. This is a means of enriching our understanding so that our understanding can bear fruit in line with the spirit. The key word is "also". This means that the thing that is understood in the intellect is the very thing that has been spoken out initially in tongues. Speaking in tongues followed by speaking in an enriched understanding is not a special anointing available to some. It is available for every believer.

Let's observe some uses of tongues from this chapter:

Tongues in Prayer

For if I pray in an unknown tongue, my spirit prayeth, but my understanding is unfruitful. What is it then? I will pray with the spirit, and I will pray with the understanding also: I will sing with the spirit, and I will sing with the understanding also.

[1 CORINTHIANS 14:14-15]

When we pray in tongues we are not praying from the capacity of our intellect but from God's. Thus we can actually pray beyond our level of soul development and beyond any limitations in our soul. God supplies us divine secrets that we then pray out. These divine secrets are not far-fetched ideas that we just blurt out. They are specific portions of God's plan for our lives though they are not immediately obvious to our minds at our current level of soul development. The utterances that are mysteries to you are not necessarily complete unknowns on the earth. They are unknown to your mind but they may be things within the grasp of other individuals who have walked further with God and learned the way of the Spirit already. When we speak them out in tongues, we are building pictures within us and as we continue to pray, over a period, we are releasing ourselves to receive the understanding of the full picture into our hearts.

Tongues in Thanksgiving

For they heard them speak with tongues, and magnify God.

[ACTS 10:46]

Speaking to yourselves in psalms and hymns and spiritual songs, singing and making melody in your heart to the Lord;

[EPHESIANS 5:19]

Spiritual songs are the products of singing with the spirit. This is the human spirit singing out fresh melodies. It is on a higher level than singing out of your understanding. No matter how much singing from your understanding touches you, singing out of your own spirit will take you much further. We know what it means to sing in the spirit because we know that he described praying in tongues as "praying with my spirit". You can let your will release your spirit's song into the physical world. Singing in the spirit is good for your whole man because the sounds are coming from the spirit, permitted through the will and completed through the mouth. In a sense, your will and your body are resonating with your spirit as they harmonize in a fresh sound. When you sing in tongues, you are simply mixing melody with the sound that flows with your tongues.

Every believer ought to develop faith in the fact that giving thanks in tongues is the best way to give thanks (1 Cor. 14:17). Giving thanks in tongues brings personal edification to us and better still to other believers who are listening to us deliver the thanksgiving in tongues, when we interpret the tongue. If you were giving thanks in tongues privately, you would be edified whether or not you interpret it. However, within a church setting, those who are standing by listening to you give thanks in tongues are not edified since it is near impossible to be edified by that which they do not understand. Our interpretation conveys the thanksgiving to the mind of the believers around us. It makes sense that the interpretation of a tongue of thanksgiving will also be thanksgiving. We should have this type of interpretation of tongues in our midst more often. It is something every believer should be able to exercise faith for.

> *Else when thou shalt bless with the spirit, how shall he that occupieth the room of the unlearned say Amen at thy giving of thanks, seeing he understandeth not what thou sayest? For thou verily givest thanks well, but the other is not edified.*

[1 CORINTHIANS 14:16-17]

The context for this thanksgiving is in a setting where those who are uninformed might not be able to say "Amen" at the giving of our thanks. This means that Paul was not discussing private giving of thanks. He was giving an instruction concerning thanksgiving in a corporate sense. It is the community of saints listening to one of the saints as he gives thanks. When you give thanks in tongues, it is not you that those standing by do not understand. The tongue is unknown to their minds, so they do not understand it.

Does their inability to say "Amen" remove from the beauty of the thanksgiving? It would appear that walking in love especially towards our weaker brethren is the greatest form of thanksgiving and properly completes the thanksgiving that we just uttered through other tongues. When our brethren are unable to say "Amen", they are not ready to release their faith to receive the miracle working dynamics of God that was made available through thanksgiving. There is power in praise that brings benefit not only to God but to the saints as well. Though that miracle-working power is around, the inability of the other saints to say "Amen" stops the group from receiving the full benefit of thanksgiving. The individual who spoke out his thanksgiving in tongues is clearly edified but the group is not. There is such a thing as receiving edification as a group.

Singing in Tongues

What is it then? I will pray with the spirit, and I will pray with the understanding also: I will sing with the spirit, and I will sing with the understanding also.

[1 CORINTHIANS 14:15]

When he said, "I will pray with the spirit", he was contrasting it with praying with the understanding, which is praying your understanding of God's Word in your normal everyday vernacular. Up till that verse, every other time that he said something was spoken while the understanding was unfruitful, he means something was spoken in unknown tongues. Therefore that expression "pray with the spirit", is praying beyond your understanding, which means it is praying with tongues.

By extension when he says, "I will sing with the spirit", what does it mean? He means singing in tongues. Speaking is the launch pad and not the landing pad for supernatural utterances. It is the beginning. You should sing in tongues a whole lot more. There is natural speech and natural singing. Nobody thinks it weird that people who can speak can also sing. We should not find it weird that there is speaking in tongues and singing in tongues. Singing in tongues simply means expressing your tongues in song form. You sing in tongues by adding melody and rhythm to what is being uttered in tongues. It is up to you to speak or sing in tongues, for that is what is meant by, "I will". God is not the one pressuring you to speak or sing in tongues. It is a decision that allows the will to release the edification of tongues.

That expression, "Praying with the spirit and praying with the understanding also", could simply mean that you are choosing to pray in tongues as well as pray in your understanding of God's Word. Paul prioritizes praying in tongues over praying in your understanding of God's Word. It would appear that if you first pray in tongues, you would ultimately be able to pray better in your understanding of God's Word. It is my opinion that when Paul said, "I will pray in the understanding also", he means that he usually prays in tongues first and he stays yielded to the Holy Spirit. The Holy Ghost will often inspire him to then pray out in a known language some of what he has previously prayed in tongues.

It is unlikely that you will receive interpretation for every prayer that you pray in tongues. This is to be expected when you consider that according to Isaiah, speaking in tongues "is the rest wherewith ye may cause the weary to rest" (Isaiah 28:12). There are things that we pray out in other tongues that if our minds were to know about could withdraw our ability to stay calm. Sometimes, where your mind is concerned, you are able to walk in peace because you do not know the specifics, though you know you have the victory in your spirit. There are things that your spirit is relaxed about but your soul is not developed enough to handle. The best way to have rest in that scenario is that your mind is kept in the dark but your spirit has the victory and it is all going to be well. When he prays out in a known language what he had previously prayed in tongues, he is praying in his understanding also.

Praying in tongues is the rest (Isa. 28:12). What are you resting on? You are resting on the faith that Jesus has authored within you (Heb. 12:2). As you pray in tongues you are not making the faith come, for faith comes by hearing God's Word (Rom. 10:17). Just to be clear, praying in tongues definitely does not supply faith. Jesus supplies faith, while you supply the speech in unknown tongues. This builds you up on the most holy faith. When you are built up on your faith, this produces peace and rest.

By two or three

If any man speak in an unknown tongue, let it be by two, or at the most by three, and that by course; and let one interpret.

[1 CORINTHIANS 14:27-28]

He is describing unknown tongues that require interpretation. This is not the "prayer language" or tongues spoken in private but a message spoken out for the whole assembly to hear and which should be promptly followed with interpretation. Some think "two or three" refers to the number of messages, while others see it as referring to the number of people participating in giving messages in tongues.

That expression, "If any man speak", refers to any Spirit-filled believer who speaks a message to be interpreted in an unknown tongue. The Holy Spirit is giving instructions about the administration of "messages" in tongues in a church service. There are those that have a ministry of diversities of tongues. They will be used of God a lot in a New Testament Church service and will definitely not be limited to two or three utterances in tongues per service. They will tend to be more prolific in utterance. They should submit their ministry to the leadership of the local assembly. Space should then be given them to operate as ministers of God. I believe that this instruction "two or three" cannot be referring to those that have a ministry along the lines of tongues and interpretation. As permitted, they would speak as often as necessary within one service until they convey the full mind of God for the service and the congregation. This verse is therefore instructing the pastor of a church to keep tabs on how many messages are permissible for "any man" or the typical believer. Typically, it should not be more than three people in a given service. If there is more to be said, we can trust God to say it through these three for a given service.

Tongues delivered in chunks

If any man speak in an unknown tongue, let it be by two, or at the most by three, and that by course; and let one interpret. But if there be no interpreter, let him keep silence in the church; and let him speak to himself, and to God.

[1 CORINTHIANS 14:27-28]

What does this, "let him keep silence in the church" mean?

This is not describing private tongues. This is a Church setting where other believers are present and there is a message to be delivered in tongues. Whenever this happens, the delivery in tongues should be followed by interpretation. One possibility is that this describes a saint who completely delivers a message in tongues, and then waits for someone to interpret only to discover that there is uneasy silence of no interpretation because no interpreter is present? This cannot be the case because the instruction implies that the fellow who starts to speak in tongues should then keep silence in the church. He would naturally keep silence if he has completed the "message" in tongues, won't he? The implication is that "messages" in tongues are to be given in chunks and not everything delivered all at once. This person starts giving a message in tongues, pauses for someone who is used in the public interpretation of tongues to interpret only to find that there is uneasy silence of no interpretation because no interpreter is present. This instruction means that the one talking in tongues should choose not to continue because the silence implies that there is no interpreter. He is not to continue giving any message in tongues except he is going to follow it up with the interpretation.

The instruction is to allow these utterance gifts to be exercised "by course". The implication of speaking by course and taking turns would mean that those who minister this way should gather together and plan the administration of the tongues in a particular service in advance. No one that is used this way needs to leave this to chance. They don't just blurt out of their mouths anything they want to say whenever they want to say it. They follow the agreed protocol for the service. Thus, no one who is used along these lines should accuse the Holy Spirit of making them blurt out things without deferring to the leadership of a service.

Let him keep silence in the Church

This instruction to "let him keep silence in the church" does not teach that the one speaking in tongues should keep quiet altogether, for he then says, "let him speak to himself and to God". Thus the fellow is silent with respect to the Church but is still speaking so softly that only he can hear himself. The implication is that we should raise our voice when switching from private tongues to tongues to be used for delivery of a message to the whole assembly. The increase in the volume of your voice should be adequate enough for the Church to distinctly pick up what you are saying. How loud is loud enough? There are no hard and fast rules about this but one thing is certain. You don't deliver a message in tongues with the same pitch of voice that you use to speak in tongues in your everyday life in private. You have other people in mind, therefore love causes you to project accordingly.

It appears that the intention of this command "let him keep silence in the church", is to the end that the fellow who has lowered his voice so that the congregation cannot hear while he is talking to himself and to God, has edified himself. There is evidence that speaking this way to himself and to God would aid him to then bring forth the interpretation of that which he has started to say in tongues. In simple terms, he does not back down and say to himself that it is futile to continue. He edifies himself to interpret the tongue, even if he is not usually the one who interprets. You can release your faith for such interpretations. This is because the principle that governs all utterance manifestations of the spirit is to pursue a course of action that best demonstrates love in all situations. A person less developed in the love walk would have backed down and apologized to the saints gathered. This is better than cooking up an interpretation. One who is highly developed in his love walk understands that there is power within the love of God to bring out the interpretation. In these matters, it is not just up to God. He has told us to desire earnestly, the best gifts as a church.

The idea of lowering one's voice in the church so as to speak to oneself and to God has certain applications for tongues in private. During a Church service, it is possible to speak in tongues softly under your breath so as not to disturb others. In that scenario, you would be getting edified from what's going on in the service at the same time drinking from the river of edification from within.

Subordinating the gift

Paul's epistle was a strong correction to the saints at Corinth to deliver them from their ignorance. They did not understand that the gifts were to be subordinated. They did not subordinate the gift to the love of God, thus they abused God's intention to use this gift to build and edify the brethren. They also did not understand the subordination of the gift to the will of the speaker, so they were disorderly and blurted out whatever they felt should be said without submitting to the leadership of the service. Thirdly, they did not subordinate this gift to the gift of interpretation of tongues when they "ministered" to the congregation. Therefore, while the speaker got some benefit, the church was not edified. These were signs of immaturity that needed correction. We must not label people in ways that the Spirit of God did not direct the bible writers to label them. Paul did not say that because of the abuses at Corinth these Corinthians were unbelievers. He still insisted that they were saints and he wrote to them as those who were sanctified in Christ Jesus.

Learning the love law of the New Covenant

Else when thou shalt bless with the spirit, how shall he that occupieth

*the room of the unlearned say Amen at thy giving of thanks, seeing
he understandeth not what thou sayest? For thou verily givest thanks
well, but the other is not edified. I thank my God, I speak with tongues
more than ye all: Yet in the church I had rather speak five words with
my understanding, that by my voice I might teach others also, than ten
thousand words in an unknown tongue.*

[1 CORINTHIANS 14:16-19]

The Bible teaches us to exercise restraint in the presence of the
unlearned. These are people that either do not see eye to eye with
us on the exercise of tongues, don't believe it is for today or who are
untrained in the ways of the Spirit.

We do not do all that can be done in the presence of the unlearned.
If we do, we can cause more harm than good. If an anointing comes
upon you to pray for someone but you are in the company of those
who are illiterate in the things of the spirit, the proper thing to
do is excuse yourself and find an appropriate place to yield to the
prompting of the Holy Ghost. It is true that if you speak in tongues
in the presence of those who are unlearned you will get a benefit but
since they are not edified find something else you can do with them
that will edify you both. If you really must get edified without them,
then speak in tongues very softly under your breath. It is bad manners
and poor spiritual etiquette to speak in tongues so loudly it distracts
others whether they are unlearned or not. Since the bible teaches us to
"seek that you may excel to the edifying of the church" (1 Cor. 14:12),
we should seek mutual edification and not just personal edification
when others are around. If I was in the presence of a tongue talking
friend and I sensed to pray, I would ask him to tag along and we can
cover more miles in the spirit together and get the job done faster. If
he is unable to join in, I would not berate him and cause him to feel
condemned for not joining me since I realize that I am not a spiritual
thermometer. My friend might rightly choose to prioritize other things
that he has on his agenda. The love of God within me does not insist
upon its own right.

What you believe is important

He that believeth on me, as the scripture hath said, out of his belly shall flow rivers of living water. (But this spake he of the Spirit, which they that believe on him should receive: for the Holy Ghost was not yet given; because that Jesus was not yet glorified.)

[JOHN 8:38]

The Lord Jesus gives us a key along these lines when He prophesied about the Church age, just before He went to the cross. He shows the pivotal nature of our believing on Him and the release of God's glory. Faith in God's ability within you will cause the river within you to flow. Don't get hung up on which gifts of the Spirit are yours, for that is really not as important as some folks make it out to be. When we compartmentalize these gifts and convince ourselves that we don't have the gifts, we shut down our yieldedness in that area. The result is that even if God wanted those manifestations to flow out through us on occasion, we are so convinced that we cannot be thus used that we become dull to His promptings. If you forget anything, do not forget that you have Christ. You have believed on Him for salvation, now you are to keep on believing on Him for the expression of God through you. You have the Giver, and the Giver of the gifts has all the gifts and can express all or any of them through you as you stay yielded to Him. Spend your time meditating on the ability of God's love within you to meet any need, at any time. If the meeting of the need calls for a manifestation of the Spirit, so be it.

You will go farther in this supernatural life, if you focus on the compassion of God than on which gifts you think you qualify or don't qualify for per se. Jesus qualifies you for everything anyway. The river within is still and stagnant until faith is released to cause its flow. It's not that God is less willing at some times and more willing at other times. We are the ones that switch off and on depending on what we believe. What you believe about what God will do or not do through you is the greatest hindrance to getting used of God. If you believe that you cannot flow in supernatural utterance you will find your experience lining up with your belief. Your will, acting as judge, will disallow you from experiencing the supernatural flow of utterance. Your unbelief stifles the flow and prevents both you and those in your world from drinking from the river within you. The river of God is full of water and it runs deep within, but it takes faith to draw upon that river for it to flow out. The love of God can reach out through you to give whatever is needed for the hour whether tongues or interpretation. The love-conscious is able to unleash the mighty potential of the spirit realm for the benefit of all.

Let no man despise thy youth; but be thou an example of the believers, in word, in conversation, in charity, in spirit, in faith, in purity.

[1 TIMOTHY 4:12]

Paul did not tell the Church not to despise Timothy's youth. He told Timothy to do something about it. The principle is that we are not always aware that we control how people perceive us. Sometimes in trying to remain contemporary and "post-modern", we try too much to blend with the world until we really are examples to unbelievers. God has not asked us to primarily be examples to unbelievers but examples to believers. Our output of excellence by the Spirit will cause the non-believer to scratch their heads. You don't have to be a mere man that's so easy for the world to figure out. You are not out to shock them. You are to live as the habitation of God.